Introduction

Welcome to New Readers Press's *Voyager 5*. In this book, you will build your reading, writing, listening, and speaking skills. You will improve your understanding of what you read. You will work with familiar types of reading selections such as stories, articles, poems, and letters. You will also work with everyday forms, documents, and graphics.

This book has four units. Each unit is based on a theme that reflects our day-to-day lives. In *Voyager 5,* you will be exploring these themes:

- ▶ Money Matters
- ▶ On the Job
- ▶ Making a Difference
- ▶ Many Cultures

Within each theme-based unit, you will find three lessons. Each lesson has the following features:

- ▶ **Before You Read:** a strategy to help you understand what you read
- ▶ **Reading:** an article, story, poem, biography, letter, memo, fable, diary entry, or essay written by adults, for adults
- ▶ **After You Read:** questions and activities about the reading
- ▶ **Think About It:** a reading skill that will help you understand what you read
- ▶ **Write About It:** an activity to improve your writing skills
- ▶ **Life Skill:** an activity to help you understand and interpret real-life reading material

We hope you enjoy exploring the themes and mastering the skills found in *Voyager 5*. We also invite you to continue your studies with the next book in our series, *Voyager 6.*

Student Self-Assessment #1

Before you begin the Skills Preview, do this self-assessment.
Share your responses with your instructor.

Reading	Good at this	Need help	Don't know how to do this
I can read and understand			
1. stories, poems, biographies, fables, and essays			
2. articles in magazines, newspapers, and books			
3. forms, applications, checks, and bank statements			
4. charts and graphs; signs and symbols			
5. diagrams and maps			
6. memos, letters, and diary entries			
7. brochures and announcements			
When I read, I can			
1. figure out new words by using context clues			
2. use what I already know to help me understand			
3. set a purpose for reading			
4. skim to get a general idea of the reading material			
5. identify main ideas and details, problems and solutions			
6. categorize information			
7. make inferences			
8. follow steps in a process			
9. recognize facts and opinions			
10. summarize what I've read			
11. try to predict what is coming next			
12. compare and contrast information			

Writing	Good at this	Need help	Don't know how to do this
I can fill out or write			
1. an action plan and instructions			
2. forms and applications; memos and letters			
3. paragraphs with a topic sentence and supporting details			
4. short articles, personal accounts, and diary entries			
5. an autobiography; fables; essays			
When I write, I can			
1. think of good ideas and organize them			
2. use facts, examples, or reasons to support my main ideas			
3. express myself clearly so others understand			
4. revise my writing to improve it			
5. edit my writing to correct spelling, capitalization, punctuation, and usage errors			
6. make subjects and verbs agree			
7. combine related ideas			

MAIN LIBRARY
ALBANY PUBLIC LIBRARY

Reading and Writing for Today's Adults

Voyager

5

Susan Paull McShane

Advisers to the Series

Mary Dunn Siedow
Director
North Carolina Literacy Resource Center
Raleigh, NC

Linda Thistlethwaite
Associate Director
The Central Illinois Adult Education Service Center
Western Illinois University
Macomb, IL

Reviewer

Ralph Galvin
Director
The Family Place
Baltimore, MD

New Readers Press

MAIN LIBRARY
ALBANY PUBLIC LIBRARY

Acknowledgments

Carruthers, Bob, "I'm Not Making Coffee," NEW AUTHORS LIBRARY, Vol. 5, Spring 1994. Reprinted by permission of the Literacy Council of Greater St. Louis.

Greer, Rebecca E. Reprinted from "What's Eating Your Paycheck" from WOMAN'S DAY Magazine by permission of Rebecca E. Greer.

Kooser, Ted. "Myrtle" from ONE WORLD AT A TIME, by Ted Kooser, © 1985. Reprinted by permission of the University of Pittsburgh Press.

Kopelnitsky, Raimonda, and Kelli Pryor. From NO WORDS TO SAY GOODBYE by Raimonda Kopelnitsky and Kelli Pryor. Copyright © 1994, Raimonda Kopelnitsky and Kelli Pryor. Reprinted by permission of Hyperion and the William Morris Agency, Inc. on behalf of the Author.

La Mar, David, "What I Do at Work," NEW AUTHORS LIBRARY, Vol. 4, February 1993. Reprinted by permission of the Literacy Council of Greater St. Louis.

Males, Carolyn. Excerpted and adapted with permission from "$100 Dreams" by Carolyn Males (READER'S DIGEST, May 1991).

Marcum, Cathy Sneed. "Making a Difference" from MOTHER JONES Magazine, January/February 1992. Reprinted with permission from Mother Jones Magazine, © 1992, Foundation for National Progress.

Quinn, Jane Bryant. "Beating Budget-Phobia" from Money Facts® by Jane Bryant Quinn, originally published in WOMAN'S DAY, October 11, 1994. Reprinted by permission of author.

Wong, Elizabeth. From "The Struggle to Be an All-American Girl" by Elizabeth Wong, LOS ANGELES TIMES, September 7, 1980. Reprinted by permission of the author.

Voyager: Reading and Writing for Today's Adults™ Voyager 5
ISBN 1-56420-155-4
Copyright © 1999
New Readers Press
U.S. Publishing Division of Laubach Literacy International
Box 131, Syracuse, New York 13210-0131

All rights reserved. No part of this book may be reproduced or transmitted in any form or by any means, electronic or mechanical, including photocopying, recording, or by any information storage and retrieval system, without permission in writing from the publisher.

Printed in the United States of America
9 8 7 6 5 4 3

Director of Acquisitions and Development: Christina Jagger
Content Editor: Mary Hutchison
Developer: Learning Unlimited, Oak Park, IL
Developmental Editor: Karen Herzoff
Contributing Writer: Betsy Rubin
Photography: David Revette Photography, Inc.
Cover Designer: Gerald Russell
Designer: Kimbrly Koennecke
Copy Editor: Jeanna H. Walsh
Artist/Illustrator: Linda Alden
Illustrator: Pat Rapple

Contents

▶ Skills Preview

This preview will give you an idea of the kinds of readings and skills covered in this book. Before you begin Unit 1, please complete the entire preview. Then share your work with your instructor.

Reading Skills Preview

Read each passage and answer the questions that follow.

The Changing Job Scene

In the 1800s about half of all people in the U.S. worked on farms. But by the early 1900s, things had changed. Many people worked in factories.

Now the job scene is changing again. The biggest growth has been in service industry jobs. Health care, education, banking, retail sales, hotels, and restaurants all provide service jobs.

Most new job openings in the 1990s have been service jobs. Examples of service jobs are firefighters, waiters, and health-care workers. Child-care workers, car mechanics, and sales personnel are service workers, too.

New service jobs may also be found in government, but mostly at the state and local levels.

The changing job scene may mean lower wages for some workers. In the past, many factory jobs offered high pay. In contrast, many of today's service jobs pay below-average wages. Some examples are janitors, waiters, clerical workers, sales personnel, and nurse's aides.

It's not all bad news. There is a lot of work for registered nurses and truck drivers. These jobs offer good wages. And as always, workers with good skills are in demand.

Choose the best answer to each question.

1. What is the main idea of this article?
   (1) Service industry jobs are growing more than other types of jobs.
   (2) Factory jobs are declining in number.
   (3) New jobs are being created in health care and sales.
   (4) Many people will have trouble getting service jobs.

2. Which of the following would be classified as a service job?
   (1) farm worker
   (2) factory employee
   (3) miner
   (4) parking attendant

Making a Difference

Cathy Sneed Marcum

After several years of working at the jail as a counselor, I developed a serious kidney disease. I underwent two years of chemotherapy, and wound up in the hospital for four months. It looked pretty bad. While I was in the hospital, a friend brought me Steinbeck's *The Grapes of Wrath.* The book really grabbed me: These were the people I worked with: strong independent people just trying to make it and not having a way out. In the book, the key to the family turning their lives around was land, working the land. I thought, we can do this at the jail—there's an old abandoned farm next door. We can start all over again!

It was not clear I was going to live. Sheriff Hennessey, who came to see me every day, said, "Sure, Cathy, do anything you want." So I told the doctors I was going home, and I did. I went back to work. I could barely walk, but I'd waddle out to the fields with a few prisoners, and we began clearing the land. We had no tools, no experience. I remember one guy, a speed addict, huge, lots of muscles, tattoos everywhere. There was an enormous bramble bush blocking a patch of land. I said, "If we could just move this bush, that's where I want to plant." I waddled off to find a hammer. By the time I came back, this guy had started tearing the bush down with his bare hands. All he needed to hear was, "Do this and it will make a difference."

Most of the inmates are in because of crack, which is totally dehumanizing—from taking it to selling it to their brothers, their sisters. When you do horrible things to people, it scars you. It makes you unable to change, because you feel so terrible about yourself. But this program offers them the chance to give back to the community. When they get here, they can't even look you in the face. It takes about two weeks and then they'll suddenly start smiling and asking questions. The window opens.

After a couple of years, I began to feel we were literally breathing life into these people and then throwing them out the gate. Every time they came back and said, "Cathy, I'm back, and I'm so glad," it would break my heart, because I knew it was true—this was the best experience they'd had. And that can't be. It's immoral that 18-year-old kids have no hope in their lives and that jail is the best alternative.

That's when Elliot Hoffman, who owns the Bay Area bakery chain Just Desserts, suggested I turn a vacant lot near the company headquarters into a garden. He wanted to make a difference in the neighborhood, and he wanted fresh produce for his bakeries. Now I can employ people when they get out. I'm using some of the proceeds from our sales to fund a house for ex-convicts. We can now tell people that things can be different. We're not just making a pretty little garden here. We're saving lives.

Choose the best answer to each question.

3. Many inmates felt bad about themselves until they
   (1) started their own businesses
   (2) worked on the farm at the jail
   (3) made new friends in prison
   (4) kicked their drug habits

4. The author suggests that the men were glad to come back to jail because
   (1) farm work was better than life outside
   (2) they needed more drugs
   (3) they respected Cathy and the sheriff
   (4) they didn't want to work

5. After starting a farm at the jail, Cathy
   (1) found abandoned farmland nearby
   (2) got a serious kidney disease
   (3) started a garden to create real jobs
   (4) read *The Grapes of Wrath*

6. It is the author's opinion that
   (1) she had a kidney disease
   (2) ex-convicts work in the new garden
   (3) the farm program was "breathing life" into people
   (4) Elliott Hoffman owns a bakery chain

Easy Ways to Save a Little or a Lot

Do you find that your money slips away almost faster than you earn it? If so, try these tips for keeping more money in your purse or pocket.

Save on food

- Reuse coffee grounds. Add about half as much fresh coffee to the old grounds.
- Buy store brand foods instead of brand names at the grocery store. They often cost less than brand-name foods, even with coupons.
- Freeze stale bread. When you get a bagful, make your own bread crumbs.
- Pack lunches instead of buying. But watch out for serving-size packaged snacks. They are expensive.

Get around town for less

- Get car tune-ups and oil changes on time. Check tire pressure. You will save on repairs and improve gas mileage.
- Take turns with neighbors driving to the store.
- Walk to shopping and errands if possible.

Cut back on other bills

- Wash clothes in cold water.
- Turn your water heater down to 125º F.
- Save on electric bills and Laundromats. Air dry your laundry in the yard, basement, or attic.
- Don't buy birthday and holiday gifts for everyone in your family. Take turns or draw names.
- Set dollar limits for gifts.

When it comes to cutting costs, think about how and where you buy soft drinks. One writer found these prices in her hometown.

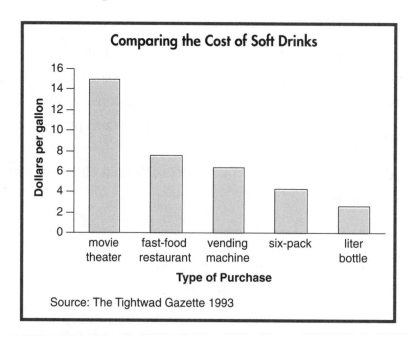

Comparing the Cost of Soft Drinks

Source: The Tightwad Gazette 1993

Choose the best answer to each question.

7. What is the main idea of this article?
   (1) Use a budget to save money.
   (2) Save money by spending less.
   (3) Rising prices make saving hard.
   (4) There are many ways to make money.

8. Based on the graph, which of these comparison statements is true?
   (1) It is cheaper to buy soft drinks in six-packs than in liter bottles.
   (2) The most expensive place to buy soft drinks is at a fast-food restaurant.
   (3) Buying soft drinks at movie theaters is more than twice as expensive as buying them from vending machines.
   (4) Buying soft drinks from vending machines is more than twice as expensive as buying them in six-packs.

9. In which category would you put an idea for homemade snacks?
   (1) save money on food
   (2) spend less on transportation
   (3) cut back on clothing costs
   (4) save on heating bills

10. The tips in this article may solve problems in
    (1) career planning
    (2) meal planning
    (3) time management
    (4) money management

Write About It

On a separate piece of paper, write about the topic below. Use the Revising Checklist to check your draft. Then give your draft to your instructor for feedback.

Topic Write one or two paragraphs about the importance of understanding other cultures. Include details from your experiences with people of other ethnic or cultural groups.

Revising Checklist

Revise your draft. Check that your draft
   _____ includes your important ideas about other cultures
   _____ has a topic sentence in each paragraph
   _____ has details to explain your experiences with other cultural groups

Skills Preview Answers

Reading Skills Preview

1.	(1)	**6.**	(3)
2.	(4)	**7.**	(2)
3.	(2)	**8.**	(3)
4.	(1)	**9.**	(1)
5.	(3)	**10.**	(4)

Write About It

Make changes on your first draft to improve your writing. Then recopy your draft and share it with your instructor.

Skills Chart

The questions in the Skills Preview assess familiarity with the following skills:

Question	Skill
1	identify main idea and details
2	understand categories
3	recognize problems and solutions
4	make inferences
5	understand sequence
6	identify facts and opinions
7	identify main idea and details
8	compare and contrast
9	understand categories
10	recognize problems and solutions

Unit 1 Money Matters

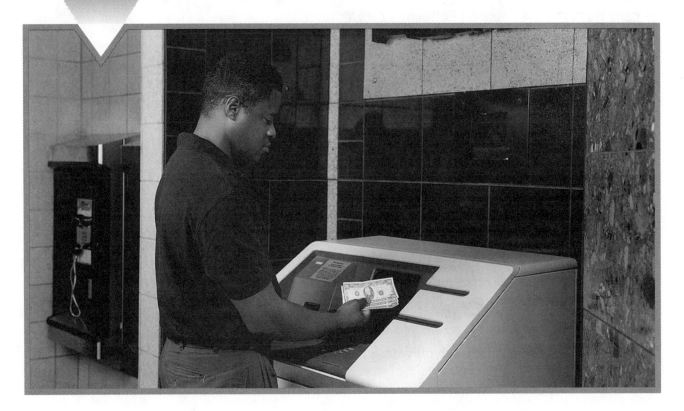

It takes money to get the things we need and the things we want. That's why money matters to all of us. Do you ever have trouble paying your bills? Would you like to save more and spend less? Do you have dreams and goals? Do you need money to make some of them real? If so, you're like most people.

Before you read Unit 1, think about your own money situation. You can learn how to make the most of your money by reading many kinds of printed information. What would you like to learn about managing your money?

▶ **Be an Active Reader**

As you read the selections in this unit
- Put a question mark (?) by things you do not understand.
- <u>Underline</u> words you do not know. Try to use context clues to figure them out.

After you read each selection in this unit
- Reread sections you marked with a question mark (?). If they still do not make sense, discuss them with a partner or your instructor.
- Look at words you <u>underlined</u>. Discuss any words you still don't understand with a partner or your instructor, or look them up in a dictionary.

Lesson 1

▶ LEARNING GOALS

Strategy: Set a purpose
Reading: Read an article
Skill: Identify the main idea and details
Writing: Write an action plan
Life Skill: Read a circle graph

Before You Read

The article "What's Eating Your Paycheck?" is about solving money problems. Before you begin the article, you should **set a purpose** for your reading. To set a purpose, consider what you would like to learn from the article. To do this, think about how you spend your money. Do you sometimes run out of money before you get paid again? On the lines below list two or three expenses you would like to reduce.

_____   _____   _____

Preview the Reading

Before you read the article, preview it by reading the title and all the headings. Think about what the headings mean.

What happens to a house of cards? What is this section probably about? Think about the headings "I deserve it" and "Dollar Dribbling." What do they suggest about spending habits?

► **Use the Strategy**
This article is about solving money problems. It offers tips for cutting back on spending. As you read the article, look for ways to reduce the expenses you listed on page 14.

What's Eating Your Paycheck?

Rebecca E. Greer

If your paycheck seems to be disappearing into thin air, you may be stuck in money traps. But don't despair; most people can get unstuck without hiding from creditors or filing for bankruptcy.

Budget Blunders

The biggest one: no budget at all. As one reader put it, "We just put all the bills in a pile, then try to decide which to pay." As she and others have learned, however, the money usually runs out before the bills do. Or as another woman wrote: "There's too much month left at the end of the money."

The same problem plagues[1] many who do have a budget. In letter after letter we read, "It looks good on paper, but it never seems to work." Why not? Often because the budgets are unrealistic.

The solution: Make a detailed record of where all your money goes now; then study it carefully. Look for expenses that can be cut back so you'll have more money for savings, vacations, and other goals. And don't give up in the face of high "fixed" expenses. Many of these can be reduced too. In fact, it's often easier to save on essentials than on enjoyable extras.

If housing takes more than 25 percent of your income, for example, consider refinancing your mortgage at a lower rate, moving to a cheaper place, or renting out an extra room. If utility bills are high, get the whole family involved in a conservation plan.

---

1. **plague:** to annoy, worry.

Some bills can be eliminated altogether. When one mother realized that cable TV was costing her $500 a year, for example, she decided that network TV wasn't so bad. If you question every expense, you can find a few that can be reduced.

◀ Check-in

Think about how to use these ideas. Which idea seems easiest for you to do? Why?

House of Cards

The costliest money trap is the credit-card bill that's never paid off. Creditors make this easy by setting minimum payments of as little as 2 percent of the total bill. But according to American Express, it will take more than 11 years (at 18.5 percent interest) to pay off a $2,000 bill with minimum payments. But many people admitted paying the bare minimum each month. Some are doing it on as many as 10 or 12 different accounts.

Interest also inflates[2] the cost of everything you buy on credit. The TV set that seemed like a terrific bargain at $300, for example, may cost $500 by the time the bill is paid off. Credit cards tempt you to buy more, too. One supermarket cashier told us she can always spot customers who plan to pay with plastic. "They buy more costly items," she said, "and pay less attention to weekly specials."

The solution: You don't have to cancel all your credit cards. Just leave them at home except when you need one for an emergency or a special purchase. You may be amazed at how much less you'll buy when you have to fork over cash.

In the meantime, concentrate on paying down those bills. Take on a second job for a while. Hold a garage sale. Sell your outgrown clothing or other unused items through a consignment shop. Start a home business marketing your crafts.

If your debts are already too high to handle, seek free or low-cost help at the nearest Consumer Credit Counseling Service. Check your telephone directory or call 800-388-CCCS.

---

2. inflate: to expand, increase.

Check-in ▶ Your purpose was to look for ways to solve money problems. Why do people spend less money when they leave their credit cards home?

Convenience-store Capers

It's no accident that most gas stations have convenience stores attached. Few of us can fill up the tank without buying a few snacks, cigarettes, lottery tickets, soft drinks, chewing gum, or other items we can live without. In fact, an Iowa woman admitted spending $50 a week at the convenience store. That adds up to $2,600 per year.

The solution: Take only enough cash for gas. Or find a station that doesn't sell anything else.

"I deserve it."

That's what hard-working men and women say to justify their lavish vacations, big stereo systems, or regular restaurant meals. They do deserve such indulgences. However, they also deserve a home of their own, a secure retirement, and freedom from worrying about unpaid bills. No one should have to live with what a Texas mother described as "constant stress, tension, even fear about money."

Sadly, the pleasure that comes from extravagances often disappears long before the bills do. The camcorder that one single mother bought for a special occasion, for example, is not much fun now. She's figured out that it will take her another three years to pay it off at $30 a month. And the New Yorkers who splurged on an outdoor hot tub now admit that they rarely use it "because we can't afford to heat it in winter."

The solution: Set priorities. Add up the annual cost of each item; then consider what else you could buy with the same money. That will help you decide which items are really worth it.

One Chicago woman, for example, discovered that daily lunches (averaging $8 each) with co-workers were costing her $2,000 a year. She decided to brown-bag it instead. "I now put twenty dollars a week into my vacation fund and another twenty into retirement savings," she says. "Those mean more to me than lunch."

Dollar Dribbling

"It's only two or three dollars," we say as we put coins into a vending machine, pick up a lottery ticket, or put off returning those videotapes. But if you save $3 a day instead of spending it frivolously, you'd have more than $1,000 at the end of the year.

The solution: Keep track of every dime you spend on little things so you can see how quickly they add up. Stop the dollar drain by removing all extra cash from your wallet every day.

▶ Final Check-in

Which of the ideas in this article might help solve your money problems? Why?

How Much Does a Car or Truck Cost?

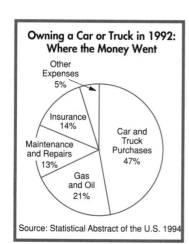

Owning a Car or Truck in 1992: Where the Money Went

Other Expenses 5%
Insurance 14%
Maintenance and Repairs 13%
Gas and Oil 21%
Car and Truck Purchases 47%

Source: Statistical Abstract of the U.S. 1994

The article you just read recommends that everyone have a budget. In order to make a budget, you need to know how much you spend. For example, there are a number of costs involved in owning a car or truck. Look at the circle graph at the left to see what those costs are. The whole circle stands for 100 percent of the costs of owning a car or truck. The sections of the circle show what percent go toward each type of expense. All the percents added up will total 100 percent.

Compare the sizes of the sections of the circle. Which section is the largest? That type of expense costs the most. What is the next most expensive item?

Purchasing the vehicle is the largest expense on the chart; gas and oil accounts for the next largest cost. If you own a car or truck, how does this information compare with your expenses? As you can see from the graph, the expense of owning a vehicle is complicated enough to require a budget all its own.

After You Read

A. Comprehension Check Choose the best answer.

1. Even so-called "fixed" expenses can be
   (1) eliminated
   (2) increased
   (3) ignored
   (4) reduced

2. The author thinks everyone should
   (1) stop using cable TV
   (2) use a realistic budget
   (3) call a credit counseling service
   (4) shop at convenience stores

3. Why are credit cards expensive?
   (1) Minimum payments are high.
   (2) Purchases have higher price tags.
   (3) You pay interest on your purchases.
   (4) You buy less with a credit card.

4. This article is composed of a series of
   (1) problems and solutions
   (2) dates and other facts
   (3) amusing stories about money
   (4) events in time order

5. What percent of the total amount of money spent on cars in 1992 went toward insurance?
   (1) 20%   (2) 12%   (3) 14%   (4) 44%

B. Revisit the Reading Strategy Can you use the ideas in this article to reduce the expenses you listed on page 14? How could you save on each expense?

_____

_____

_____

C. Think Beyond the Reading Think about these questions and discuss them with a partner. Answer the questions in writing if you wish.

- What must you do to stick to a budget? What skills and habits do you need?
- Which of your expenses are necessary? Of those expenses that are not necessary, which are the most important to you? How do you budget for entertainment or fun?

Think About It: Identify the Main Idea and Details

When you read the article "What's Eating Your Paycheck?" you may have asked, "What's the point?" The "point" of a reading selection is the **main idea**—what the selection is about. Sometimes the author states the main idea of a selection in a topic sentence. It is often the first or second sentence of the selection. The main idea of this article appears in the second sentence: ". . . most people can get unstuck without hiding from creditors or filing for bankruptcy."

The rest of the article discusses common problems and suggests solutions. Each paragraph has its own main idea, which relates to the main idea of the article. Most paragraphs contain a topic sentence that states the main idea of the paragraph. The rest of the paragraph contains **details**—facts, examples, or reasons that support or explain the main idea.

A. Look at Identifying the Main Idea and Details

Look at the example from the article. Notice how the main idea of the paragraph is stated in the underlined topic sentence.

> ▶ <u>In the meantime, concentrate on paying down those bills.</u> Take on a second job for a while. Hold a garage sale. Sell your outgrown clothing or other unused items through a consignment shop. Start a home business marketing your crafts.

Now number the four details in the paragraph. Each detail is an example of how to earn extra money to pay your bills.

B. Practice Read each paragraph and underline the topic sentence. Then answer the questions.

1. ▶ Some bills can be eliminated altogether. When one mother realized that cable TV was costing her $500 a year, for example, she decided that network TV wasn't so bad. If you question every expense, you can find a few that can be reduced.

   State the main idea in your own words by finishing this sentence.

   You can get rid of _____

   _____

2. ▶ Sadly, the pleasure that comes from extravagances often disappears long before the bills do. The camcorder that one single mother bought for a special occasion, for example, is not much fun now. She's figured out that it will take her another three years to pay it off at $30 a month. And the New Yorkers who splurged on an outdoor hot tub now admit that they rarely use it "because we can't afford to heat it in winter."

State the main idea in your own words by finishing this sentence.

The fun of buying expensive things _____

_____

3. ▶ The costliest money trap is the credit-card bill that's never paid off. Creditors make this easy by setting minimum payments of as little as 2 percent of the total bill. But according to American Express, it will take more than 11 years (at 18.5 percent interest) to pay off a $2,000 bill with minimum payments. But many readers admitted paying the bare minimum each month. Some are doing it on as many as 10 or 12 different accounts.

Write one detail from the paragraph that supports or explains the main idea.

_____

Talk About It
Summarize this article for a friend or family member. When you summarize, you give the most important information. First state the main idea of the article. Then use the headings in the article to identify the important details—the major problems and their solutions. Discuss other ideas for managing money.

Write About It: Write an Action Plan

The article "What's Eating Your Paycheck?" may have given you some ideas for saving money. Write about how you plan to spend less.

A. **Prewriting** Think of a way you can cut back on spending. Then write an action plan for doing it. For example, you may decide to spend less money on food. Brainstorm possible ways you can reduce food spending, listing every idea that comes to mind. Use your own ideas and ideas from the article. Here is an example:

> Cut back spending by: <u>Spending less on food.</u>
> Action Plan
>
> • <u>Use coupons</u>   • <u>Make a budget</u>
>
> • <u>Make homemade snacks</u>   • <u>Eat out less often</u>

Use the lines below to write your own action plan.

> Cut back spending by: _____
> Action Plan:
>
> • _____
>
> • _____
>
> • _____

B. **Writing** Write a paragraph that explains your action plan.

- Write a topic sentence that states the goal of your action plan. For example: "To save money, I will spend less on food."
- Then write details that include examples for saving money. Explain what you will do, when, and how.

▶ **Save your draft.** At the end of this unit, you will choose one of your drafts to work with further.

Life Skill: A Closer Look at Reading a Circle Graph

In order to save money, you have to know how you are spending it. The circle graph below shows how most people in the U.S. spent their money in 1992. Circle graphs, also called pie charts, show numbers or amounts as parts of a whole. The circle stands for all, or 100 percent, of something. The parts are shown as percents of the whole circle. The percent of a section determines its size.

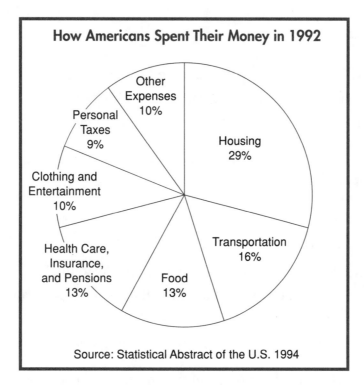

How Americans Spent Their Money in 1992

- Other Expenses 10%
- Personal Taxes 9%
- Clothing and Entertainment 10%
- Health Care, Insurance, and Pensions 13%
- Food 13%
- Transportation 16%
- Housing 29%

Source: Statistical Abstract of the U.S. 1994

To understand this graph, first read the title. Then see how the sections of the circle compare to each other. The largest "slice" is labeled "housing." Reading the percentages confirms that housing is the biggest expense.

What percent of spending was for food? _____

You are correct if you said that 13 percent was spent on food.

Practice Read the graph and answer these questions.

1. What percent of spending was for transportation? _____

2. What percent was for clothes and entertainment? _____

3. Add together spending for housing, transportation, and food.

   What percent was for these three basic expenses? _____

Lesson 2

LEARNING GOALS

Strategy: Skim reading material
Reading: Read a chart and bank signature card
Skill: Understand categories
Writing: Fill out a bank signature card
Life Skill: Read a bank statement

Before You Read

In this lesson, you will read about how one couple opened a checking account. But first, think about what you already know about checking accounts and banking. Write any words that come to mind below.

_____

_____

Preview the Reading

To preview "Opening a Checking Account," skim the material. When you **skim,** you read the title, the headings, and any words in bold type. Skim the text, the chart, and the signature card. You may also want to read the first sentence in each paragraph.

Read the bold print on the chart. What is the chart about? What do you think the purpose of the signature card is?

▶ **Use the Strategy**
You skimmed the article to get the "big picture"—an idea of what the article is about. You also saw that there are three different kinds of material in the article: text, a chart, and a filled-in form. Now, guided by what you learned from skimming, read to find more details.

Opening a Checking Account

Jon Williams has never had a bank account before. But now he is married and has a new job. He and his wife, Sherry, want to start keeping their money in a bank.

When he went to the bank he was surprised. He told Sherry, "When you open a checking account, it's like shopping. You choose the services you need. The man at the bank said to read this chart and choose the plan that is right for us."

Types of Checking Accounts		
Plan	**Benefits**	**Fees**
Special Checking ($25 to open)	◆ open with only $25 ◆ 5 free checks per month	◆ $3.00 monthly service charge ◆ $.50 for each check over 5
Personal Checking ($100 to open)	◆ unlimited free checks ◆ no fee to use bank's automated teller machine (ATM)	◆ $8.00 monthly service charge ◆ no fee when you keep a $750 daily balance or $1,500 in savings
EARN Checking with Interest ($200 to open)	◆ unlimited free checks ◆ no fee to use bank's ATM ◆ pays 2% interest	◆ $8.00 monthly service charge ◆ no fee when you keep a $1,500 daily balance or $2,000 in savings

Check-in

Jon and Sherry estimated the number of checks they would write each month. Between home expenses and personal spending, they realized they might write as many as 25 checks in a month. They decided the Special Checking account would cost too much. It had a check charge and a service charge. The EARN account would require them to keep too much money in the bank. They chose the Personal Checking account because the $8.00 service charge would be cheaper than paying $.50 per check.

Have you opened an account at a bank? Is your account similar to one of the three in the chart? If so, which one?

Jon and Sherry went together to open their checking account. The bank gave them an account number and a booklet called *Deposit Account Regulations* that described the bank's rules. Then Jon and Sherry filled out the signature card below.

Bank Signature Card

Account Name 1			Soc. Sec. No.
Jonathan R. Williams			000 – 00 – 0000*

Address
711 River Drive, Apt. 2B

City	State	Zip	Telephone
Benton	Arkansas	72015	(501) 555 – 9362

Employer
City Bus Company

Account Name 2			Soc. Sec. No.
Sherry J. Williams			000 – 00 – 0000*

Checking Account Type:

Special Checking ____ Personal Checking _✔_ EARN ____

Account Number: _____90151268_____

> **Customer Agreement:** I agree to the rules of the bank that apply to my accounts. I have received a copy of the Deposit Account Rules. Under penalties of perjury,[1] I certify[2] that the Social Security number on this form is my correct taxpayer identification number.

Signature(s)

1. *Jonathan Williams*   2. *Sherry J. Williams*

---

*This example uses zeros instead of a real Social Security number.
1. **perjury:** lying under oath.   2. **certify:** to guarantee as true.

Jon and Sherry wrote their names on the lines marked "Account Name 1" and "Account Name 2" so that both of their names would be on the account. Then they filled out the other information. Finally, Jon and Sherry read the Customer Agreement and signed the card.

▶ **Final Check-in**

Do you always read a document before signing it?
Why is that a good idea?

After You Read

A. Comprehension Check

1. Which plans have no monthly fee if you keep a minimum balance in your account? _____

2. What is the monthly service charge for the Special Checking account?

   _____

3. How much money must you keep in the Personal Checking account to avoid paying the monthly service charge? _____

4. How much interest does an EARN account currently pay? _____

5. What should Jon and Sherry read to find information about the bank's rules? _____

6. What important personal numbers did Jon and Sherry write on the signature card? _____

B. Revisit the Reading Strategy

1. Skim the chart again and write what ATM means. _____

   _____

2. Write one other thing you learned when you skimmed the chart and form. _____

C. Think Beyond the Reading
Think about these questions and discuss them with a partner. Answer the questions in writing if you wish.

- Do you have a checking account? If so, how does it help you to manage your money? If not, would you like to open an account? Why or why not?
- What questions would you ask a bank representative if you decided to open a checking account?

Think About It: Understand Categories

Grouping similar things together is a way of organizing information to make it easier to understand. Grouping similar things together is called classifying. The first step in classifying is to identify the groups or **categories** into which items will be grouped. Similar things are then placed into the same category.

Charts and graphs are often used to group and display information in categories.

A. Look at Understanding Categories

Charts classify information by putting it into columns and rows. Chart categories are named in column or row headings. What are the three categories of information in this chart?

Types of Checking Accounts		
Plan	Benefits	Fees
Special Checking ($25 to open)	◆ open with only $25 ◆ 5 free checks per month	◆ $3.00 monthly service charge ◆ $.50 for each check over 5
Personal Checking ($100 to open)	◆ unlimited free checks ◆ no fee to use bank's automated teller machine (ATM)	◆ $8.00 monthly service charge ◆ no fee when you keep a $750 daily balance or $1,500 in savings
EARN Checking with Interest ($200 to open)	◆ unlimited free checks ◆ no fee to use bank's ATM ◆ pays 2% interest	◆ $8.00 monthly service charge ◆ no fee when you keep a $1,500 daily balance or $2,000 in savings

The categories are Plan, Benefits, and Fees. These headings tell you what type of information appears in each column.

B. Practice Reread the chart on page 28 and the graph below and answer the questions.

1. In which category would you look to find how much interest you can

   earn on your checking account? _____

2. In which category would you look to find the deposit amount

   required to open each type of account? _____

3. In which category would you look to learn how much money you

   need to keep in the bank to avoid a service charge? _____

Graphs also present information. Here is the circle graph from page 23.
Each section of the graph represents a category of spending.

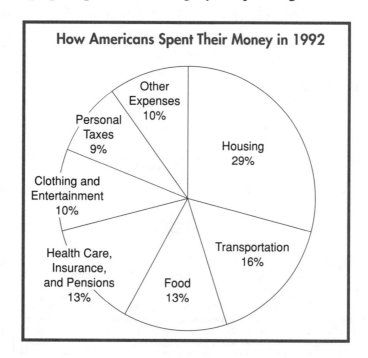

How Americans Spent Their Money in 1992

4. In which category did Americans spend the most money?_____

5. In which category did Americans spend the least money? _____

▶ **Talk About It**

Take turns with a partner to act out the roles of a bank employee and a customer opening an account. As the bank employee, explain the types of accounts. As the customer, ask questions about one type of account. If you were to open a checking account at this bank, which type of account would you choose and why?

Write About It: Fill Out a Bank Signature Card

Like Jon and Sherry, you will probably open a checking account at some time in your life, if you haven't already. In order to fill out the bank's signature card, you will need to be sure of some information.

A. Prewriting Before you start, make sure you have the information you need to fill out the form. You may want to make a list of your Social Security number and the other information requested on the form.

B. Writing Fill out the form below. Print on all but the signature lines. Write your Social Security number under the abbreviation "Soc. Sec. No." Place a check beside the name of the checking account that would be best for you. The account number is filled in for you. Read the Customer Agreement carefully. Then sign your name after number 1 on the last line.

Bank Signature Card

Account Name 1   Soc. Sec. No.

_____

Address

_____

City   State   Zip   Telephone

_____

Employer

_____

Account Name 2   Soc. Sec. No.

_____

Checking Account Type:
Special Checking _____   Personal Checking _____   EARN _____
Account Number: _____ 90151270 _____

> **Customer Agreement:** I agree to the rules of the bank that apply to my accounts. I have received a copy of the Deposit Account Rules. Under penalties of perjury,[1] I certify[2] that the Social Security number on this form is my correct taxpayer identification number.

Signature(s)

1. _____   2. _____

---

1. **perjury:** lying under oath.   2. **certify:** to guarantee as true.

Life Skill: Read a Bank Statement

To help you manage your money in a checking account, the bank sends you
a statement every month. The statement is a list of checks, withdrawals,
and deposits made to your account that month.

Study the account statement below.

COUNTY BANK

Personal Checking Account Statement   Statement Date: 6-30-98
Carol Ramirez   Account Number:123-4567

Account Summary

Beginning Balance	1,575.68	Deposits	1,308.48
Checks/Deductions	1,135.60	Ending Balance	1,748.56
Fees	0.00		

Transactions	Date	Amount	
Check 1051	6-1	550.00	
Check 1052	6-1	31.65	
Check 1055	6-3	50.00	
Deposit	6-7		327.12
Check 1054	6-8	102.95	
Check 1053	6-10	225.00	
Check 1056	6-13	22.00	
Deposit	6-14		327.12
Check 1060	6-14	36.50	
Check 1058	6-16	17.00	
Deposit	6-21		327.12
Withdrawal-ATM Main St.	6-23	50.00	
Check 1057	6-25	18.50	
Check 1059	6-25	32.00	
Deposit	6-28		327.12
Fees	6-30	0.00	

Practice On separate paper, answer the questions about the account statement.

1. How much money did Carol withdraw on June 23? _____

2. What was the total amount of checks and other deductions for the month? _____

3. What happened on June 28? _____

4. How much money was in the account at the end of the month? _____

Lesson 3

LEARNING GOALS

Strategy: Use your prior experience
Reading: Read an article
Skill: Recognize problems and solutions
Writing: Write a short article
Life Skill: Understand a budget

Before You Read

The article "$100 Dreams" is about the Trickle Up Program (TUP), which gives people around the world $100 grants to start their own businesses. You can use your **prior experience**—your personal experiences—to help you understand what you read. What are your dreams? What would you do if someone offered you $100 to start your own business? Discuss your ideas with a partner or a small group.

Preview the Reading

The events in this article take place all around the world. To preview the article, find these places on a world map or a globe:

Nepal	Andes Mountains	Kenya
Cameroon	Caribbean Islands	Philippines
Ecuador	Dominica	

▶ **Use the Strategy**

As you read, think about whether the Trickle Up Program would help you or someone you know to start a business.

$100 Dreams

Carolyn Males

Three and a half years ago, Pancha Maya, her husband and five children lived in a ramshackle flat in southern Nepal. Every morning the parents walked the dirt roads, seeking work in the rice fields. After the harvest, the family went begging for food.

Today the Mayas own a small paper-bag-making company. Their work space is the front yard of the new bamboo house they own. With the money they've earned, the Mayas have purchased a small plot on which they grow vegetables and raise goats for additional income. In fact, the family has saved 1,700 rupees ($68). This is remarkable in a country with a per-capita income of $160.

Grace Mbakwa, her husband and eight children once lived hand-to-mouth in the cattle town of Tugi, Cameroon. Today the Mbakwas run a clothing manufacturing business and own a home. They are able to send their children to school—at a costly annual sum of $2,800.

The idea of starting her own business seemed impossible to Pilar Moya, a poor woman from Atahualpa, high in Ecuador's Andes Mountains. Today, however, she is one of the proud owners of a bakery specializing in sweet cakes.

These businesses are part of an economic revolution sweeping the developing world. The catalyst[1] is the Trickle Up Program (TUP), an ingenious[2] nonprofit organization founded by New Yorkers Glen and Mildred Leet. TUP offers people like the Mayas, the Mbakwas and the Moyas modest $100 grants. Since 1979, the program has helped over 130,000 of the world's neediest people in 90 countries win small, lifesaving victories over poverty. And it has turned conventional thinking about foreign aid on its head.

---

1. catalyst: something that acts to bring about change.   **2. ingenious:** clever.

Poor Planning

During distinguished careers in international development, the Leets had seen that billions of dollars pouring into Third World welfare programs were not reaching those who needed help. Corrupt officials took their cut. Bureaucracies devoured the rest. What money the poor did get only made them more dependent.

Even well-intentioned projects were often poorly planned and executed. The Leets once visited a Caribbean-island place mat factory. They expected to see the much-touted modern machinery purchased with foreign aid. Instead they found 10 workers huddled in a vast room, stitching the coconut fiber by hand. Dozens of new sewing machines nearby lay idle, covered with dust.

"Why aren't you using your machines?" Glen asked the women. "We have electricity only one day a week," they replied. Planners hadn't considered the cost of gasoline to power the generators. So the plant's output remained the same.

In your experience, what is the best way to give help to people who need it?

◀ Check-in

The Leets concluded that there must be a better way. Wouldn't it make more sense to offer small grants to start cottage industries[3] and services and let the dollars "trickle up?" Then, step aside as individuals use their own skills and initiative to pull themselves out of poverty. That would cut out the fat-cat middlemen.[4] It would also cut out complicated grant applications and regulations that drain resources, energy and enthusiasm. Skeptics jeered. Fight global poverty with $100 grants? Ridiculous! It was like aiming with a pea shooter at a giant.

Heads Up

Undaunted, the Leets put their theory to the test on the Caribbean island of Dominica. They outlined TUP's requirements to a group of locals:

---

3. **cottage industry:** a small manufacturing business carried on at home.
4. **fat-cat middlemen:** traders who buy cheaply from producers and sell to retailers at much higher prices.

Get five or more people together. Decide what kind of a business you want, and draw up a marketing plan with a TUP coordinator's assistance. TUP will send a $50 start-up check. Within three months, put 1,000 hours of work into your company, keeping records of sales. Reinvest 20 percent of the profits. Fill out a one-page business report form. TUP will mail a second $50. After that, you're on your own. No more money. No exceptions.

Check-in ▶ Does this plan sound as if it would work for you? Why or why not?

"Some listeners looked incredulous," Millie recalls. "But there were two or three whose eyes lit up." At the port town of Marigot, the Leets met with five poor women who were eager to start their own business. Marigot, one woman explained, had a big plant, where South American bananas, bound for Europe, were crated. "If one banana is spoiled," she said, "they throw out the entire bunch."

"Is there anything you can make with the bananas?" the Leets asked.

"We thought we might make banana chips to sell in grocery stores," another replied. Strangely, even as the conversation grew more animated, the women kept their heads down.

"How much is your work worth per hour?" Glen asked. The group seemed baffled by the question. "It's not worth anything," murmured Myld Riviere. Millie persisted. "Okay, if someone paid you for this work, how much would it be?" About one dollar, Myld estimated. "Well, if you put in a thousand hours in your business, that's $1,000," Glen pointed out. Suddenly, the women's eyes lifted. A *thousand dollars?* Their time had value!

Soon the Leets, who still take no salary, moved on to Jamaica, Montserrat, St. Kitts and Barbados.[5] They set up office in their New York apartment, filling file cabinets with TUP business plans and reports. Fired up by the couple's successes, government and social-development agencies, corporations, philanthropic[6] foundations and friends began sending contributions. With the money came volunteers—nearly 3,000 since the program began.

---

5. **Jamaica . . . Barbados:** islands in the Caribbean.
6. **philanthropic:** giving aid to promote human welfare.

. . . Success is measured not just in money, but in the new self-confidence on the faces of TUP's beneficiaries.[7] It's dressmaker, Grace Mbakwa from Cameroon, pointing with pride to her Paid Business License on the wall of her shop. It's 50 women from a squatter settlement near Nairobi, Kenya, marching en masse to open savings accounts. It's Pancha Maya, who once wore rags, standing tall in her lovely red sari among neighbors in Nepal. Even the names many TUP grantees choose for their businesses— The New Hope, Marching Together, The Progressive Five— reflect their new-found strength.

In 1989, Millie returned to Dominica. She found the banana-chip company still in business, although much had changed after almost ten years. It was now housed in a two-room factory. When Millie knocked, Myld Riviere opened the door, a broad smile on her face. Boldly extending her hand and looking Millie in the eye, she was no longer the shy, unskilled woman who valued her labor at nothing.

Report Card

. . . Clearly, Trickle Up has helped the poor dare to dream. One of the best illustrations of this occurred in the Philippines when Millie visited a sausage-making company headed by Carlota Yambot. Just before leaving, she asked Carlota's children what they wanted to be. "A lawyer," said the 17-year-old daughter. "A pharmacist," said the 15-year-old son. "A foreign-service worker," said the 13-year-old. Clutching Millie's arm, Carlota smiled and said, "We all have dreams, but now because of Trickle Up, we have hope."

---

7. **beneficiary:** someone who receives a benefit or advantage.

▶ **Final Check-in**
You know how it feels to be successful at something. How did success affect the people in the article? Did their businesses have to make millions of dollars to be successful?

After You Read

A. Comprehension Check

1. Why did the Leets start TUP?
   (1) Foreign aid projects often didn't work.
   (2) They couldn't afford a big aid project.
   (3) Government leaders asked for their help.
   (4) People weren't working hard enough.

2. The Trickle Up Program gives money to
   (1) large foreign aid projects
   (2) successful businesses
   (3) poor people
   (4) foreign governments

3. Why wasn't the machinery donated to the place mat factory used?
   (1) It was broken.
   (2) There wasn't enough machinery.
   (3) It was sent to the wrong factory.
   (4) They didn't have the electricity to use it.

4. Many people didn't think TUP would work because
   (1) it was poorly managed
   (2) $100 was not enough money
   (3) corrupt officials would take the money
   (4) poor people couldn't run a business

B. Revisit the Reading Strategy
Using your experience, react to these statements. Discuss your reactions with a partner or a group.

Yes	No	Maybe	
_____	_____	_____	1. A program like TUP would work in America.
_____	_____	_____	2. People should be helped to help themselves.
_____	_____	_____	3. Even against the odds, dreams can come true.

C. Think Beyond the Reading
Think about these questions and discuss them with a partner. Answer the questions in writing if you wish.

- Do you have an important dream or goal? If so, do you think you can achieve it? What strengths and skills do you have that will help you achieve it?
- What kind of help, if any, do you need to reach your goal?

Think About It: Recognize Problems and Solutions

Helping people solve their problems is a popular topic in newspapers, magazines, and books. This type of article usually begins by identifying and explaining a problem, and then offering one or more solutions. To understand these articles, you must be able to apply the skill called **recognizing problems and solutions.**

A. Look at Recognizing Problems and Solutions

1. The people in the excerpt below from "$100 Dreams" had a serious money problem. They couldn't earn enough to live:

   ▶ Three and a half years ago, Pancha Maya, her husband and five children lived in a ramshackle flat in southern Nepal. Every morning the parents walked the dirt roads, seeking work in the rice fields. After the harvest, the family went begging for food.

   The Maya family's solution is found in the following excerpt:

   ▶ These businesses are part of an economic revolution sweeping the developing world. The catalyst is the Trickle Up Program (TUP), an ingenious nonprofit organization founded by New Yorkers Glen and Mildred Leet. TUP offers people like the Mayas, the Mbakwas and the Moyas modest $100 grants.

   The solution was that the Mayas started their own successful business.

2. Find the problem and its solution in the next passage:

   ▶ Grace Mbakwa, her husband and eight children once lived hand-to-mouth in the cattle town of Tugi, Cameroon. Today the Mbakwas run a clothing manufacturing business and own a home. They are able to send their children to school—at a costly annual sum of $2,800.

   The problem was that the Mbakwa family lived hand-to-mouth.
   The solution was for the Mbakwas to run a business.

B. Practice Read the excerpts and answer the questions.

1. ▶ . . . the Leets had seen that billions of dollars pouring into Third World welfare programs were not reaching those who needed help. Corrupt officials took their cut. Bureaucracies devoured the rest.

   Underline the sentence that best states the problem.

2. ▶ Wouldn't it make more sense to offer small grants to start cottage industries and services and let the dollars "trickle up?" Then, step aside as individuals use their own skills and initiative to pull themselves out of poverty.

   What is the solution offered in the excerpt above? _____

   _____

3. ▶ The idea of starting her own business seemed impossible to Pilar Moya, a poor woman from Atahualpa, high in Ecuador's Andes Mountains. Today, however, she is one of the proud owners of a bakery specializing in sweet cakes.

   a. What is the problem in the passage? _____

   b. What was the solution? _____

   _____

 Talk About It
Discuss the kind of business you could start in order to make money.
- How much money would you need to start this business?
- What would you spend the money on?
- What skills would you need to make this business a success?

Write About It: Write a Short Article

"$100 Dreams" is about poor people who become business owners. Now you will write some ideas for affordable businesses.

A. Prewriting Interview people who run a business at home or who operate their business at very low cost. For example, some people make items at home and sell them to stores. Others run lawn-mowing or cleaning services with low overhead costs. Ask questions such as these:

- How much money does it cost to set up this business?
- What skills do you need to run this business?

Person: Gina H.

Type of Business:
lawn mowing service

Start-up Costs:
cost of mowers
$100 per week for advertising
gas, oil, maintenance

Skills needed to run this business:
willingness to work long hours
ability to keep track of income and expenses
ability to fix lawn mowers
ability to accurately estimate how long a job will take

B. Writing Write a two-paragraph news article about your interviews. Use the notes you took in part A.

1. In the first paragraph, describe your questions and the interview process. How many people did you talk to? What questions did you ask?
2. In the second paragraph, summarize the answers, using two or three examples. What kinds of businesses do people run from home? What kinds of businesses have low costs? How much do these businesses cost to start and operate? What do you need to know in order to run these businesses?

▶ **Save your draft.** At the end of this unit, you will choose one of your drafts to work with further.

Life Skill: Understand a Budget

A **budget** is a plan for spending your money. To make a budget, you predict your expenses. Total expenses should be less than monthly income. Below is part of a sample budget. Compare this person's actual spending with the amount budgeted. In what expenses did the person spend more than the budgeted amount this month?

Expense	Monthly Budgeted Amount	Actual Amount Spent
Rent	475.00	475.00
Electricity	60.00	75.00
Groceries	200.00	180.00
Eating Out	40.00	66.00

You were right if you said this person spent more than was budgeted for electricity and eating out.

Practice Read the categories in this sample budget for a family of four. Then answer the questions on separate paper.

Monthly Income 1,500.00	Expense	Monthly Budgeted Amount	Actual Amount Spent
	1. Food	200.00	230.00
	2. Housing	675.00	675.00
	3. Transportation	50.00	70.00
	4. Entertainment	35.00	55.00
	5. Clothing	75.00	30.00
	6. Insurance	200.00	200.00
	7. Savings	265.00	240.00
		1,500.00	1,500.00

1. How much did the family plan to save?
2. How much did they save?
3. Did they spend more than they budgeted for entertainment?
4. What is the family's total monthly income?
5. Did they stay within their budget for the month?
6. For which two items did the family spend exactly the amount budgeted?
7. Why were they able to predict the amounts for these two items accurately?
8. Why were they unable to predict amounts in the other categories as accurately?

▶ Writing Skills Mini-Lesson: Capitalization Rules

Use a **capital letter** at the beginning of these words:

1. **The first word of a sentence and the word *I*.**
    > My husband and **I** want a car. **We** are saving for a new one.

2. **Days of the week, holidays, and months.**
    > Tuesday, Saturday, Thanksgiving, the Fourth of July, March, June

> **Tip** Do not capitalize small words like *the, a, of,* or *and*.

3. **Names of places such as cities, states, countries, and continents.**
    > Detroit, Michigan, Japan, Europe

4. **Names of organizations, institutions, companies, and brands.**
    > the American Cancer Society, University of Delaware,
    > Ford Motor Company, Kleenex

5. **People's titles and names.**
    > Mr. Martin Pagano, Ms. Carla Raymundo, Mrs. Vista, Ted Beck,
    > Dr. Albert Choi, Professor Sykes, Senator Feinstein

> **Tip** Capitalize people's titles only when they are used with the person's name. Do not capitalize them when they appear alone:
> I like **Professor Rashid.** She is an excellent **professor.**

Practice This paragraph has no capital letters. Find the words that should start with a capital letter. Then copy the paragraph on your own paper, capitalizing words correctly.

> when i shop, i always compare prices. for example, i usually use
> tide for my wash, but last monday i got ivory since it was on sale. i
> also compare prices for services. when i moved to chicago last april,
> my friend jamal told me about two good doctors. i chose dr. angela
> carter at grant hospital because she charges less than the other doctor.

Reading Review

Being a Smart Borrower

Think carefully before you borrow money. Taking out a loan can help solve some problems. But paying off a debt can be expensive. Borrow only when you really need extra money right away.

For example, you might need to make major repairs to your car. Or your child might need a lot of dental work. For problems like these, you need a lot of money quickly. A loan might be the answer.

People also borrow for large purchases and long-term goals. This allows you to use an item you buy while you are paying for it. For instance, most people take out a loan to buy a car or a house. And many people borrow to cover the cost of job training or college.

It's best not to take on a big debt unless you really need to. Before borrowing, ask yourself these questions:

- Do I really need to buy this now?
- Is it still a good deal when the interest (cost of borrowing money) is added to the price of the item?
- Can I afford the payments?

If you answer "no" to any of these questions, a loan might *cause* more problems than it solves.

If you decide to borrow, shop around for the best loan for you. Check with different banks. Ask about different types of loans. Get the lowest interest rate you can find. Here are some terms to know:

- **principal:** the amount you borrow
- **interest:** the charge for borrowing money—usually a percent of the principal
- **loan:** the amount you borrow plus the interest
- **collateral:** something that the lender accepts as security in case you don't make your loan payments. This may be the item you are buying. The car is often the collateral on a car loan.

Finally, get all of your questions answered. Be sure you understand the fine print on any loan contract before you sign it. Ask about your right to change your mind. Be a smart borrower.

Choose the best answer to each question.

1. What is the main idea of this article?
   (1) Interest rates make borrowing easy.
   (2) It is important to be a careful borrower.
   (3) You should always invest your money.
   (4) You should avoid borrowing money.

2. The article says if you need a lot of money right away, one solution is to
   (1) get a loan
   (2) look for a second job
   (3) look for a high interest rate
   (4) save for a rainy day

3. When you borrow money, you pay
   (1) collateral
   (2) interest
   (3) credit
   (4) security

4. Which of the following would be classified as a long-term need?
   (1) a new dress
   (2) dinner at a restaurant
   (3) a house
   (4) holiday shopping

Writing Process

In Unit 1, you wrote two first drafts. Choose the piece that you would like to work with further. You will revise, edit, and make a final copy of this draft.

_____ your action plan for cutting back on spending (page 22)

_____ your article about ideas for new businesses (page 40)

Find the first draft you chose. Then turn to page 160 in this book. Follow steps 3, 4, and 5 in the Writing Process to create a final draft.

As you revise, check your draft for these specific points:

Action plan: Did you suggest specific solutions to your money problem?

Article: Did you give examples from your interviews?

Unit 2 On the Job

Work is an important part of life. Sometimes work is satisfying. Sometimes it just makes you tired. But whether you go to a job every day or work at home, you do important work. You help to support and take care of yourself and your family. You work to keep your home clean and safe. And you work to learn new things every day.

Sometimes you learn new skills and ideas from others. Sometimes you figure things out for yourself. Before you begin Unit 2, think about the different kinds of work you do. Think about other people's jobs, too. What makes work satisfying? What is your idea of a good job?

▶ **Be an Active Reader**

As you read the selections in this unit
- Put a question mark (?) by things you do not understand.
- <u>Underline</u> words you do not know. Try to use context clues to figure them out.

After you read each selection in this unit
- Reread sections you marked with a question mark (?). If they still do not make sense, discuss them with a partner or your instructor.
- Look at words you underlined. Discuss any words you still don't understand with a partner or your instructor, or look them up in a dictionary.

Lesson 4

LEARNING GOALS

Strategy: Imagine
Reading: Read personal accounts and a poem
Skill: Make inferences
Writing: Write a personal account
Life Skill: Read workplace signs and symbols

Before You Read

Two readings in this lesson, "I'm Not Making Coffee" and "What I Do at Work," are personal accounts of work experiences. Both were written by students at the Literacy Council of Greater St. Louis. The third reading, a poem entitled "Myrtle," is about a woman and her job.

To understand other people's stories, it helps to imagine yourself in their place. To see how this works, think of someone you saw working today— for example, a road repair worker, a mail carrier, or your child's teacher. Imagine yourself doing that person's job. Think about it and then answer the questions below.

When does your imaginary workday begin? _____

Who do you work with? _____

How does your work make you feel? _____

Preview the Reading

Skim "I'm Not Making Coffee" and the poem "Myrtle." Look at the pictures. Try to figure out what kind of work these people do. Now predict what you think you will learn about them and their jobs.

I'm Not Making Coffee

Bob Carruthers

One day I picked up a lady. She got in the cab and told me where she was going. I started the meter and off we went.

Let me explain something to you. This lady was a very nice elderly lady.

We got to her house and I had about $6.45 on the meter. The lady paid me and gave me a tip. I got out of the cab and opened the door to help her out. She asked if I would carry her bags to the door. I said, "Okay" and I did.

I came back to the cab to get her and help her up the steps. We got to the front door and stopped. She turned to me and said, "Would you mind opening the door for me?" I said, "Okay." At that, she handed me the keys. I opened the door, and held it open for her. At last, she stepped into the house.

Then she asked me if I would set her bags inside the door. Again I said, "Okay." As I set the bags down, she asked if I would turn on the lamp for her, and again I said, "Okay."

As I turned for the door, I heard her voice say, "Would you help me untie my coat? I have arthritis very bad." Once again, I said, "Okay."

Finally I said, "Hey lady! I have to go back to work sometime today." And she said, "That's okay, I'm not going to make coffee."

> **Check-in**
> Did you imagine yourself in the cabdriver's place? How did you feel about the woman? Angry? Amused? Surprised? Impatient?

Myrtle

Ted Kooser

Wearing her yellow rubber slicker,

Myrtle, our *Journal* carrier,

has come early through rain and darkness

to bring us the news.

A woman of thirty or so, with three small children at home,

she's told me she likes

a long walk by herself in the morning.

And with pride in her work,

she's wrapped the news neatly in plastic—

a bread bag, beaded with rain,

that reads WONDER.

From my doorway I watch her

flicker from porch to porch as she goes,

a yellow candle flame

no wind or weather dare extinguish.

► **Check-in**
Did you imagine yourself doing Myrtle's job? How did you feel walking in the rain in the early morning? Would you enjoy Myrtle's job? Why or why not?

After You Read

A. Comprehension Check

1. What is Bob Carruthers' job? _____

2. Write two things the passenger in Bob's story asked him to do.

   _____

   _____

3. How many times did Bob tell the lady, "Okay"? _____

4. Besides delivering newspapers, what other work does Myrtle do?

   _____

5. What makes the poet think that Myrtle takes pride in her work?

   _____

B. Revisit the Reading Strategy You were asked to imagine yourself doing Bob's and Myrtle's jobs. Remember how you felt as you read. Also think about how you imagined Bob and Myrtle felt. Check whether you agree or disagree with these statements.

Agree	Disagree	
_____	_____	1. Bob didn't really want to help the passenger.
_____	_____	2. Although Bob was helpful, he probably felt impatient.
_____	_____	3. Bob was probably afraid to go into the woman's house.
_____	_____	4. Myrtle may have felt like sleeping late on a rainy morning.
_____	_____	5. Myrtle enjoys her work.

C. Think Beyond the Reading Think about these questions and discuss them with a partner. Answer the questions in writing if you wish.

• Would you tip Bob? Would you tip Myrtle? What kind of worker deserves a tip?

• Do you like work that involves helping people? Why or why not?

Think About It: Make Inferences

When you **make inferences,** you use clues to figure out something that isn't actually stated in words. You do this every day, when you use your knowledge and experience to "fill in the missing pieces"—make sense of what you see and hear.

Making inferences is sometimes called "reading between the lines." For example, you can use the clues in the paragraph below to figure out, or **infer,** that Bob is a cabdriver.

> ▶ One day I picked up a lady. She got in the cab and told me where she was going. I started the meter and off we went.

A. Look at Making Inferences

1. When you read, you can infer how someone feels by using the clues, your experience, and your imagination. In the conversation below, how do you think Bob feels?

> ▶ Finally I said, "Hey lady! I have to go back to work sometime today."

He seems to be running out of patience. You can tell from what he says and how he says it. And you can imagine how you would feel in Bob's place.

2. Now think about the woman's reply to Bob's statement. Why do you think she says this?

> ▶ And she said, "That's okay, I'm not going to make coffee."

Here are some possible answers: She might mean that she won't need to ask Bob for more help. Or maybe she means that she would invite him in for a quick break, but not for coffee.

How might Bob react either way?

You might say that Bob would be upset if she asked for more help. Or maybe he would enjoy a break. You can see that often, more than one inference can be made.

B. Practice

1. Answer these questions about "I'm Not Making Coffee."

   a. Do you think the woman lives alone or with someone else?

   _____

   b. How many steps do you think they had to climb to get to the front door?

   _____

   c. Why do you think the woman asks the cabdriver for so much help?

   _____

2. Answer these questions about the poem "Myrtle."

   ▶ A woman of thirty or so, with three small children at home,
   she's told me she likes
   a long walk by herself in the morning.

   a. Why do you think Myrtle might enjoy a morning walk by herself?

   _____

   _____

   b. Reread the whole poem (page 48). Why do you think the poet chose
   to write about an ordinary person like Myrtle?

   _____

   _____

   ▶ **Talk About It**
   Read "I'm Not Making Coffee" or "Myrtle" aloud to a group of students,
   friends, or family members. Discuss how Bob or Myrtle feels about their
   work. Then discuss these questions with the group:
   • Do you like your job most of the time?
   • What do you like and dislike about it?
   • What would make your job more enjoyable?

Write About It: Write a Personal Account

"I'm Not Making Coffee" and "Myrtle" are about people and their jobs.
Now write about work that you do, either at a job or at home.

A. Prewriting Read the personal account below, written by David La Mar. He
describes his typical workday and lists specific tasks. Notice the details
he uses to explain his job. You can use his story as a model for your own.

What I Do at Work

David La Mar

I come in every morning at 10:00 A.M. I work all day busing
tables, cleaning and repairing the restaurant and doing just about
anything that needs to be done. I usually get off work about 5 P.M.
Lots of times I end up back at work if they beep me because of an
emergency, and there usually is one.

If I don't have to go back to work I try to do other jobs at night
or work around the house. On Saturday nights at work I make all
of the salads for the restaurant. At this time of the year the kitchen
gets so hot, way over 100 degrees. Other things I do at work
sometimes are paint, clean the kitchen, clean walls and stoves,
and unclog and replace plumbing. I do these things on Monday
when the restaurant is closed.

Now choose a topic for your own personal account. You may write about
your job or the work you do at home. Write your topic on this line.

_____

After you choose your topic, make a list of the things you do every day in
your work. It might help to write numbers beside each item to show what
you do first, second, third, and so on. List specific tasks. Then make a
second list of other responsibilities and tasks you do.

What I do every day

_____

_____

_____

_____

_____

_____

Other tasks and responsibilities

_____

_____

_____

_____

_____

_____

_____

B. Writing Write two paragraphs describing your work, using the lists you made above. In the first paragraph, describe a typical day on the job, using your first list. Tell the important things you do. For the next paragraph, use your second list. Write about your other responsibilities and other things you do. Give your writing a title. You may use a simple one like David La Mar's title, or make up something that fits your job.

▶ **Save your draft.** At the end of this unit, you will choose one of your drafts to work with further.

Life Skill: Read Workplace Signs and Symbols

Part of doing a job includes reading signs at the workplace. Signs in the workplace are very important. For example, signs can

- tell you where to find something
- identify certain places
- give a warning

A. Signs in the workplace have many purposes.

   1. Some signs give directions.

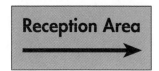

   2. Other signs identify offices or departments.

   3. Many workplace signs give instructions or warnings.

B. To understand signs, read the following terms and their meanings.

- **authorized:** having rights
- **hazard:** source of danger
- **permit:** written permission, such as a badge
- **personnel:** employees, workers
- **prohibited:** not allowed
- **required:** necessary, must have
- **toxic:** poisonous
- **voltage:** electrical power

C. Sometimes symbols instead of words are found on signs.

This symbol means prohibited, or not allowed. When something is pictured inside this symbol, the thing that is pictured is not allowed.

Practice With a partner, figure out what these signs mean. Discuss why each sign is important. Then write a sentence telling what each sign means.

1. **HAZARDOUS WASTE AREA** _____

2. **AUTHORIZED PERSONNEL ONLY** _____

3. **WARNING DOOR SWINGS OUT** _____

4. **CAUTION HIGH VOLTAGE** _____

5. **Safety First: Bend Knees When Lifting** _____

6. **HARD HAT AREA** _____

7. **CAUTION FLAMMABLE LIQUID** _____

8. **WATCH YOUR STEP** _____

9. **SLIPPERY WHEN WET** _____

10. **ENTER BY PERMIT ONLY** _____

11. **SAFETY GLASSES REQUIRED** _____

12. _____

13. _____

Lesson 5

LEARNING GOALS

Strategy: Use your prior experience
Reading: Read a work order and diagram
Skill: Follow steps in a process
Writing: Write directions
Life Skill: Read a diagram

Before You Read

"First Day on the Job: The Self-Taught Plumber" tells how a man uses a diagram to teach himself how to make a repair. Have you ever used a diagram that showed you how to do something? If so, your **prior experience** can help you understand this reading selection.

Have you ever taken something apart to repair it, or put parts together to

build something? If so, what? _____

How did you know what to do? (Check one or more.)

_____ I watched someone else do it.   _____ I figured it out by looking at the item.

_____ Someone told me what to do.   _____ I looked at the diagrams.

_____ I read the directions.   _____ I used trial and error.

Preview the Reading

Look at the picture and skim the next two pages. What kind of work will you be reading about? Look at the diagrams and the work order. Make a mental note of anything that you will need to study carefully.

Use the Strategy

You will read about how Miguel fixed a faucet that dripped. Use your prior experience with repairs, at home or on the job, to help you understand the diagram.

First Day on the Job: The Self-Taught Plumber

Miguel has a new job. He's the maintenance man at the Oakwood Manor Home for senior citizens. When he was hired, the manager said, "This old building needs a lot of repair."

Miguel was good at fixing things, but he had never done much plumbing work. He was worried about that. So he was nervous when he got a work order to fix a dripping faucet. "Oh, no! Not on the first day!" he thought. At lunch, he drove to the library to get a book on home repairs.

Here is the work order Miguel received.

Work Order

Date _7-22_   No. ___203___

Requested by ___Mrs. McCain___

Location ___Apartment 12B___   Phone ___555-7963___

Request taken by _Maria_   Date needed __7-25__

Work needed _Fix dripping faucet in kitchen sink_

_____

_____

Completed (initial and date) _____

Check-in ▶ Have you ever seen a work order before? Is it like other forms you have used? How is it the same? How is it different?

The sink in apartment 12B wasn't exactly like the one in the book, but it was close. Miguel followed the directions in the book and stopped the drip!

This is what Miguel found in the library book.

Repairing a Faucet That Has a Worn Washer

To replace a worn washer, follow these steps.

Step 1

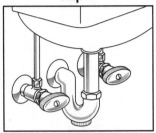

Turn off water at the shutoff valve. The shutoff is usually under the sink.

Step 2

If faucet handle covers packing nut, remove handle.

Step 3

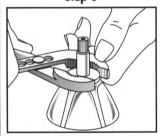

If faucet has a decorative cover, remove the cover to get at packing nut. You can put tape around the base of the fixture to avoid scratching it.

Step 4

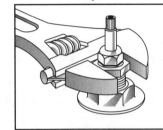

Remove packing nut by turning it counterclockwise with a wrench.

Step 5

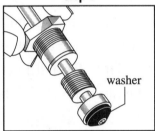

washer

Remove stem assembly.

Step 6

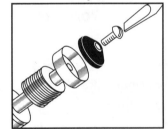

Locate the worn washer and replace it with a new one.

Step 7

Put the unit back together by reversing the order of steps 1–5 above. Remember to open the shutoff valve.

▶ **Final Check-in**

Have you ever followed written directions to repair something? Did drawings help you picture the process? If so, did you use that experience to help you understand these directions?

After You Read

A. Comprehension Check

1. What is the purpose of a work order?
   (1) It lists what services are available.
   (2) It tells a worker what to do.
   (3) It shows customers how to get help.
   (4) It tells how much to pay a worker.

2. Whose name is written on the line "Requested by"?
   (1) the person who does the work
   (2) the person who takes the call
   (3) the supervisor on the job
   (4) the person who asks for the work

3. What do you do first to repair a faucet?
   (1) Remove the handle.
   (2) Replace the worn washer.
   (3) Turn off the water.
   (4) Remove the packing nut.

4. According to the diagram, the washer is a part of the
   (1) faucet handle
   (2) decorative cover
   (3) packing nut
   (4) stem assembly

B. Revisit the Reading Strategy What strategies have you used when following written directions to assemble or repair something? Check one or more. Discuss the strategy that was most helpful to you.

_____ Read the directions aloud.

_____ Match the actual parts with those pictured on a diagram.

_____ Ask someone to help you.

_____ Check off steps as you do them.

C. Think Beyond the Reading Think about these questions and discuss them with a partner. Answer the questions in writing if you wish.

- People learn in different ways. What is your preferred strategy for learning how to do something? Discuss these different ways of learning:
  – reading directions   – watching someone do it
  – listening to directions   – doing it

- What would help you to learn more easily at school? At home? On the job?

Think About It: Follow Steps in a Process

When you follow directions, you are usually **following steps in a process.**
Directions may tell how to do something or make something. They may be
broken down into steps, which you can follow in order. So that you can
follow the steps in the correct order, they are usually numbered. The
steps may contain clue words such as *first, next, while,* and *last* that tell
you when to do each step.

Look at these steps for how to operate a fax machine. Notice the way both
numbers and clue words are used to help you do it in the right order.

How to Send a Fax

1. First, press the button labeled "Dial tone."
2. Next, place the paper facedown in the document feeder.
3. Then, dial the fax number of the person to whom you are sending the fax.
4. Last, press the button labeled "Start."

A. **Look at Following Steps in a Process**

When you follow steps in a process, it is especially important to
understand the order in which things should be done. In the example
below, what do you do after you remove the packing nut?

4. Remove packing nut by turning it counterclockwise with a wrench.
5. Remove the stem assembly.

As you can tell by the numbers, the next step is to remove the stem assembly.

B. **Practice** Answer these questions about the steps in repairing a faucet that
has a worn washer.

1. What do you have to do just before replacing the worn washer?

   _____

2. What do you do just after replacing the worn washer?

   _____

3. What two things might have to be removed before you can remove the

packing nut? _____

4. The steps below are *not* in the correct order. Write a number beside each
step to show the order in which they should be done.

_____ If faucet handle covers packing nut, remove handle.

_____ Turn off water at the shutoff valve.

_____ Remove packing nut by turning it counterclockwise with a wrench.

5. On the lines below, list in order the steps for putting the faucet back together.
The first and last steps are done for you.

1. <u>Replace the stem assembly.</u> _____

2. _____

3. _____

4. _____

5. <u>Turn the water back on.</u> _____

 Talk About It

The correct order is important when giving and following "how to"
directions. Think about the steps necessary to fix or make something
simple, such as fixing a broken window or using an automatic
camera. When giving steps in directions, how can you make your
directions clear?

As a listener, what can you do to be sure you understand and remember
the correct order? Discuss these strategies for listening to directions. Add
other strategies of your own.

• Listen for steps.

• Repeat the steps to yourself.

• Visualize the steps.

Write About It: Write Directions

Sometimes you need to write down directions as part of your job. For example, you might have to write directions for a co-worker to follow. On page 58, you saw how the steps for repairing something can be shown with diagrams. In this activity, you will write steps that explain how to make something or how to repair something. You will write your steps in a kind of diagram called a flow chart.

A. **Prewriting** Before writing directions for following steps in a process, it helps to create a flow chart for the process. A flow chart shows each step in a separate box. Arrows between the boxes show the order of the steps.

Look at this sample flow chart that shows the steps for refinishing a piece of furniture. Think about how the flow chart shows the steps of the process.

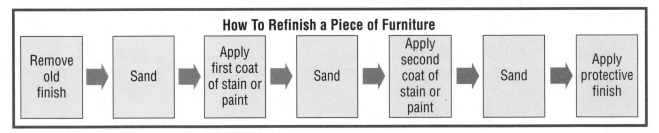

How To Refinish a Piece of Furniture

Remove old finish → Sand → Apply first coat of stain or paint → Sand → Apply second coat of stain or paint → Sand → Apply protective finish

Now think of something you do at work or at home that you would like to write directions for.

• First write a title: How to _____

• Next, on a separate paper, list the materials and equipment in the order in which they are used.

• Then make a flow chart. Write the directions in the boxes. Make sure that you write only one step in each box and that you write the steps in order.

B. **Writing** Write your directions for others to read. First write your title. Then list the materials and equipment in the order in which they are used. Finally, write the steps, following their order in your flow chart. Number each step and give necessary details to explain how to carry them out.

▶ **Save your draft.** At the end of this unit, you will choose one of your drafts to work with further.

Life Skill: Read a Diagram

The diagram that Miguel followed showed him how to do a plumbing job. Diagrams are pictures that show how to do something, how something works, or what parts something has. Study these diagrams that show how to assemble a table.

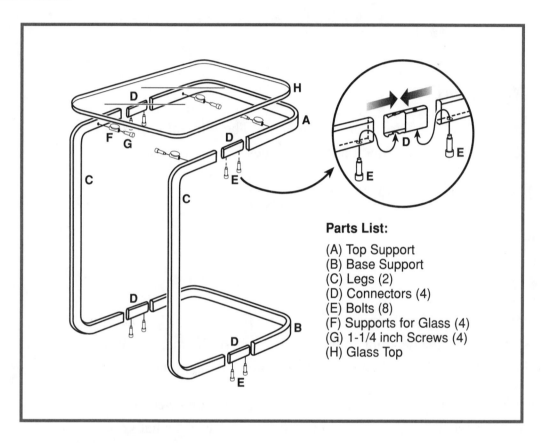

Parts List:
(A) Top Support
(B) Base Support
(C) Legs (2)
(D) Connectors (4)
(E) Bolts (8)
(F) Supports for Glass (4)
(G) 1-1/4 inch Screws (4)
(H) Glass Top

Practice Answer the questions below.

1. What part is the base? _____

2. How many legs does the table have? _____

3. The smaller diagram is an enlargement of part of the table. What does it show?

   _____

4. The bolts (E) attach part D to what other parts? _____

5. The screws (G) attach the glass supports (F) to what parts of the table? _____

   _____

6. Name at least one way parts A and B are alike. _____

Lesson 6

LEARNING GOALS

Strategy: Use your prior knowledge
Reading: Read memos
Skill: Identify facts and opinions
Writing: Write a memo
Life Skill: Read a time sheet and an invoice

Before You Read

The readings in this lesson are a series of memos. These memos are short business letters that give information to employees in a warehouse.

A memo usually begins with headings like this:

To:
From:
Date:
Subject:

Memos are usually brief and written in a businesslike style. The topic of a memo is listed under the heading "Subject." The rest of the memo gives specific information about the subject in one or more paragraphs.

To understand the readings in this lesson, use your **prior knowledge** about memos and their subjects. To practice this strategy, use what you know about work to think of possible subjects for memos. On the line below, write one reason a manager might write a memo to employees.

_____

Preview the Reading

To preview the readings, read the title and look at the pictures. Then read the memo headings. Ask yourself these things:

* Who sends the memos?
* To whom are they sent?
* What are they about?
* What do you think is going on at this company?

Use the Strategy

The purpose of these memos is to get employees to solve safety problems at work. As you read them, think about safety problems at your job or at home. How is the safety problem at this company similar to safety problems you know about? How is it different?

Problem Solving on the Job

To:	Warehouse employees
From:	Marie Bowman, General Manager
Date:	May 8
Subject:	Safety problems on the job

In the last six weeks we have had reports of two accidents. The accidents were caused by oil spills on the warehouse floor and in the storage area. Both could have been avoided by following safety procedures. It appears that safety rules are being ignored.

All employees must follow safety procedures. Remember to read directions and follow procedures at all times.

Thank you for your help with this problem.

To: Warehouse employees
From: Steve Chang, Personnel Manager
Date: June 3
Subject: Training in Problem Solving

A training course on problem solving will be offered twice this summer. The first session will begin July 8 and will meet twice a week on Monday and Wednesday evenings, for three weeks. Each class will be 5:00–7:00 P.M. The course will be repeated, beginning August 5, at the same times. Details are on the sign-up sheet outside the personnel office. Deadline for sign-up is June 24.

Both hourly and salaried employees may take the course. Management believes the training will help employees work "smarter." Further, we feel employees can use skills from this course to help solve the recent safety problems. As an added benefit, those who take the course will learn new skills to use off the job as well.

◄ **Check-in**

Based on your knowledge, why might workers want to take this training?

To: Warehouse employees
From: Steve Chang, Personnel Manager
Date: June 21
Subject: Update on problem-solving training

Don't forget to sign up for the problem-solving course by June 24.

Note that there is a change in the times. Training courses will now take place **4:00–6:00** P.M. This change in times means that part of the course will take place during work hours. Employees will be paid for one hour of each two-hour class.

As mentioned before, we think the training will be well worth the time it takes. Employees with problem-solving skills may advance in the company more quickly. Further, these skills will be useful in both work and personal settings.

◄ **Check-in**

Why might the time have been changed? Do you think more people will take the training as a result of the time change?

To:	Warehouse employees
From:	Marie Bowman, General Manager
Date:	September 10
Subject:	Congratulations on a safety problem solved

I am pleased to report that three employees have each found a way to avoid oil spills. You may recall that oil spills caused two accidents in May. The company thanks Marsha O'Brien, Tyrone Simpson, and Tony Vacarro. All three took the problem-solving course during the summer. With the skills they learned, each tackled the problem in a different way.

These fine employees will get a bonus the first of next month. They will also be the first to receive "Problem Solver of the Month" awards. Look for their names on the plaque in the front office.

Thanks again to Marsha, Tyrone, and Tony! They have made this a safer workplace.

 Final Check-in

Think about your work experience. Why would the company write this memo and give a reward to these employees?

After You Read

A. Comprehension Check

1. What is the safety problem mentioned in the first memo?

_____

2. Why is the company offering the training? Name two reasons.

_____

_____

3. Why do you think the company decided to offer part of the training

during paid working hours? _____

4. How did the company benefit from offering training to its employees?

_____

5. Do you think the employees who took the training will be able to use it

outside of work? If so, how? _____

_____

B. Revisit the Reading Strategy
Use your prior knowledge and think about
meetings you have attended. What information should be included in a
memo announcing a meeting of employees? Check each item below that you
would include. Write at least one more suggestion.

_____ date of the meeting

_____ location of the meeting

_____ purpose of the meeting

Other _____

C. Think Beyond the Reading
Think about these questions and discuss them
with a partner. Answer the questions in writing if you wish.

- How important is it to you to learn new skills through on-the-job training?
  What do you gain?
- How do you solve problems at work or at home? What strategies do you use?

Think About It: Identify Facts and Opinions

On the job and in your personal life, you need to recognize the difference between **facts** and **opinions.** This skill is important because opinions may sound like facts. For example, in ads and political campaigns opinions are often presented as facts. If you recognize them as opinions, you will not be misled about products or candidates.

A **fact** is a statement that can be shown to be real or actual.
Example: Employees took a training course.
If a statement is a **fact,** you can answer "yes" to at least one of these questions:

• Can it be seen, heard, or felt?
• Can it be looked up in a reliable source?
• Has it been supported scientifically?

An **opinion** is a statement of belief, a guess, or a prediction.
Example: I think lifelong learning is important.

Opinions have not been proven to be true. Opinion statements may use words like *think, believe, seem,* and *appear.* Some opinion statements don't use these words. They may sound like facts.
Example: The senator is the best man for the job.

A. Look at Facts and Opinions

1. In the sentences below, how can you tell which is a fact and which is an opinion?

   ▶ In the last six weeks we have had reports of two accidents.

   ▶ It appears that safety rules are being ignored.

   The first sentence is a fact because there is a record of the accidents and people saw them happen. The second sentence is an opinion because the manager is saying what she thinks has caused the problem. Notice the use of the word *appears*.

2. Which statement below is a fact? Which is an opinion?

▶ . . . we think the training will be well worth the time it takes.

▶ Details are on the sign-up sheet outside the personnel office.

The first sentence is an opinion. Notice the use of the words *we think*.
The second sentence is a fact.

B. **Practice** Read the statements below and identify the facts and opinions.
Write **F** for **Fact** or **O** for **Opinion** on the line before each statement.

_____ **1.** Management believes the training will help employees work "smarter."

_____ **2.** The accidents were caused by oil spills on the warehouse floor and in the storage area.

_____ **3.** Part of the course is now being offered during work hours.

_____ **4.** We feel it will help solve our recent safety problems.

_____ **5.** Three employees found ways to avoid oil spills that cause accidents.

_____ **6.** Employees with problem-solving skills may advance more quickly.

_____ **7.** All employees must follow safety procedures.

_____ **8.** People who take the course will benefit from it.

_____ **9.** The course will be repeated beginning August 5.

_____ **10.** Giving employees training during work hours is a good idea.

▶ **Talk About It**
When you summarize a selection, you tell only the most important points. Reread the memos. Then, with a partner or a small group, take turns summarizing each memo in this lesson. The tips below may help you. After each memo has been summarized, look back at the actual memo to see whether you covered the most important points.

Tip
• First, state the main idea, or the purpose, of the memo.
• Next, tell the important details in the memo.

Write About It: Write a Memo

In this lesson, you read memos about a problem at a company. Now you will write a memo about a problem at your job or in your neighborhood.

A. **Prewriting** First, state the problem. Then list details about the problem and some possible solutions. In the example below, a woman is planning a memo to a local government official:

Problem: Streetlights are out.

- dark streets invite crime
- dangerous to drive city streets in the dark
- government offices closed at night; can't call to report streetlights out

Possible Solutions

- provide night number for reporting streetlights out
- keep lights in better repair

The woman will probably choose to write about the first solution. Even lights in good repair can go out. A night number is the best solution because people may forget to call and report the problem the next day.

Now state your own problem. Then make a list of details about the problem and a list of possible solutions. Use the list below as a model. Decide which solution you will recommend in your memo.

Problem

_____

Possible Solutions

_____

B. **Writing** Write a two-paragraph memo to a person who can address your problem. Use the memos in this lesson as a model. Start your memo with a heading like the ones in those memos. Then use your lists for ideas:

- In the first paragraph, explain your problem. State the facts carefully. If you write an opinion, be sure to use words like *I think* or *I feel*.
- In the next paragraph, explain the solution you think is best.

▶ **Save your draft.** At the end of this unit, you will choose one of your drafts to work with further.

Life Skill: Read a Time Sheet and an Invoice

Many different forms are used in the workplace. On these two pages, you will learn how to read a time sheet and an invoice.

Time Sheet

A **time sheet** like the one below is used to record the number of hours an employee worked.

WEEKLY TIME SHEET

Name of Employee

Janet Garcia   For Week Ending 9–3

Day of Week	Morning		Afternoon		Overtime		Office Use Only	
	In	Out	In	Out	In	Out	Reg. Hrs.	Overtime
MONDAY	7:55	11:59	12:30	4:35			8.25	0
TUESDAY	7:59	12:01	12:31	4:30	4:31	5:30	8.0	1
WEDNESDAY								

Authorization of Overtime ___P. Morissard___

No Overtime Without Authorization

Employee Signature ___Janet Garcia___

Employee must <u>personally</u> fill out and sign time sheet.

At the beginning of the week, the employee fills in her name and the date. Every day she fills in her hours. She will be paid for the hours she works, rounded to the nearest quarter hour. She will not be paid for her lunch hour. Her boss must sign off on overtime at the bottom. Totals are entered by payroll personnel in the column headed "Office Use Only."

When did the employee go to lunch on Monday? When did she return?

The employee left for lunch at 11:59 A.M. and came back at 12:30 P.M.

A. **Practice** Answer the questions on separate paper.

   1. Who fills in the two columns at the far right on the time sheet?
   2. How many hours did the employee work Monday?
   3. How much overtime did the employee work so far this week?
   4. Who authorized the overtime?

Invoice

An invoice is a bill for a purchase or service. The invoice below was filled out by an employee of Stein's Office Supplies. The information on the form is in two parts. The top part is information about the customer. The bottom part is about the order. Read the invoice carefully.

INVOICE	Stein's Office Supplies		21650

SOLD TO Marvin Browning   **SHIP TO** Marvin Browning

ADDRESS 321 E. Fourth Ave.   **ADDRESS** Same

CITY, STATE, ZIP Edgerton, IA 00625   **CITY, STATE, ZIP**

SALESPERSON JPR   **TERMS** Charge-VISA   **DATE** 6-12

ORDERED	SHIPPED	DESCRIPTION	PRODUCT NO.	PRICE	UNIT	AMOUNT
5-28	6-10	Desk lamps	3079A	15.95	2	31.90
5-28	6-10	Desk chair	8504	115.49	1	115.49

B. Practice Answer the questions.

5. How much did the desk chair cost? _____

6. What terms (method of payment) did Marvin Browning choose?

_____

7. What is the product number of the desk chair? _____

8. When were the chair and lamps shipped? _____

9. How much did each desk lamp cost? _____

10. What was the total cost of the lamps? _____

▶ Writing Skills Mini-Lesson: Making Subjects and Verbs Agree

Every sentence has a **subject** (who or what the sentence is about) and a **verb** (what the subject does or is). In the present tense, verbs appear in different forms. The form of a verb changes depending on its subject. In other words, a verb must **agree** with its subject.

Follow these rules to make subjects and verbs agree in the present tense:

1. Add the *s* or *es* ending to the verb when the subject is a singular noun or the pronoun *he, she,* or *it.*

   A **carpenter** builds cabinets. **He** builds cabinets.
   A **pilot** flies planes. **She** flies planes.

2. Do not add an ending to the verb when the subject is a plural noun or the pronoun *I, you, we,* or *they.*

   Carpenters build cabinets. **I** build cabinets. **You** build cabinets.

3. The verb *to be* has several forms. See the chart below.

• I am	• we are
• you are	• you are
• he is, she is, it is	• they are
• the car is, the pilot is	• the cars are, the pilots are

Practice What do these people do on the job? Write complete and logical sentences about them.

1. Carpenters <u>build cabinets and furniture.</u>

2. A photographer _____

3. A driving instructor _____

4. Pilots _____

5. Firefighters _____

6. I _____

Reading Review

Who Needs People Skills?

Amy wore a grim look as she walked out of the office of her college adviser, Janet Driscoll. She left the building and hurried to the parking lot. In addition to taking courses for a nursing degree, Amy had a job at a department store. She didn't want to be late for work. On the way to the car, she muttered aloud, "What a waste!" Her friend Carmen was waiting in the car. She said hello, but Amy was already complaining. "Mrs. Driscoll said I absolutely have to take the communications course! Why do I need that for nursing?"

Carmen said, "I think it's a good course. I took it last spring. You practice listening and do role plays. You pretend to be solving problems on the job. It seemed practical. I think it will help me work with people."

"Well, I don't have time for it," Amy said in disgust. "I know how to listen! I just want to get my nursing degree."

At work that night, Amy forgot about the meeting with her adviser. The store was so full of holiday shoppers that she had no time to think. By the end of the night, she was tired and tense.

Just before closing, Amy's manager came to talk with her. "Amy," she said, "a customer complained about you today. She wanted to return a dress. She said you were rude."

Amy got red in the face. "I was not!" she said loudly. "She had worn that dress. I didn't think I should take the return. So I told her to ask at the office. Then she got mad. But I wasn't rude."

The manager answered quietly. "I'm not saying you were. I just came to hear your side of the story. You don't have to get upset."

"I'm not upset! I'm just telling you I didn't do anything wrong," said Amy in an angry tone.

"I understand," said the manager. "Let's talk about it tomorrow."

As they left the store, she stopped Amy. "You're a good worker," she said. "But I think you need better communication skills. On any job you have to work with people."

Amy had to smile in spite of herself. "Where have I heard that before?" she thought.

Choose the best answer to each question.

1. In the first paragraph you learned that Amy is
   (1) studying to be a nurse
   (2) teaching nursing courses
   (3) angry with Carmen
   (4) happy with her adviser

2. Which of Carmen's statements is a fact?
   (1) "I think it's a good course."
   (2) "I took it last spring."
   (3) "It seemed practical."
   (4) "I think it will help me work with people."

3. It is an opinion when the manager says
   (1) "I understand."
   (2) "She wanted to return a dress."
   (3) "I came to hear your side of the story."
   (4) "I think you need better communication skills."

4. At the end Amy thinks that
   (1) she needs the communication class after all
   (2) the customer is always right
   (3) she should quit school
   (4) she needs to work harder at her job

Writing Process

In Unit 2, you wrote three first drafts. Choose the piece that you would like to work with further. You will revise, edit, and make a final copy of this draft.

_____ personal account of the work you do (pages 52–53)
_____ directions explaining how to do something (page 62)
_____ memo about a problem at home or on the job (page 71)

Find the first draft you chose. Then turn to page 160 in this book. Follow steps 3, 4, and 5 in the Writing Process to create a final draft.

As you revise, check your draft for these specific points:

Personal account: Have you included details that explain the work you do?
Instructions: Did you check that all the steps are in order?
Memo: Have you suggested solutions for the problem?

Unit 3 Making a Difference

Most of us believe that we have a responsibility to others. We see people around us who need help. We know about problems in our own neighborhoods and cities, as well as problems our nation faces. We would like to be able to make a difference.

In this unit you will read about Shirley Chisholm, a woman who made a difference at the national level. You will also read about how ordinary citizens can make a difference in their communities. As you read, think about these questions: What are the needs in your community? How can you help? Does your vote matter? How can your voice be heard?

▶ Be an Active Reader

As you read the selections in this unit
- Put a question mark (?) by things you do not understand.
- <u>Underline</u> words you do not know. Try to use context clues to figure them out.

After you read each selection in this unit
- Reread sections you marked with a question mark (?). If they still do not make sense, discuss them with a partner or your instructor.
- Look at words you <u>underlined</u>. Discuss any words you still don't understand with a partner or your instructor, or look them up in a dictionary.

Lesson 7

LEARNING GOALS

Strategy: Predict content
Reading: Read a biography
Skill: Summarize information
Writing: Write an autobiography
Life Skill: Read a brochure

Before You Read

The reading selection in this lesson is a biography of Shirley Chisholm. A biography is the story of a real person's life. Chisholm was the first black woman to become a member of the United States Congress. Like all members of Congress, she was elected by people in her home district. She stood up for their needs and interests as she helped make laws to govern the country. The biography shows how her early life prepared her for this important work.

As you read, use the strategy of **predicting content.** When you predict content, you try to foresee what will happen or what will come next. Practice the strategy now. What kind of information do you expect to find in a person's life story? One idea is already suggested below. Write two more predictions of what you might learn in a biography.

Date of birth _____

_____

_____

Preview the Reading

Preview "Shirley Chisholm: First Black Congresswoman" by looking at the pictures and reading the section headings. Then read the first and last paragraphs. What do you think you will learn in this story about Chisholm's career in Congress?

▶ **Use the Strategy**

Predict what kinds of problems you think Shirley Chisholm might have faced while running for public office.

Shirley Chisholm: First Black Congresswoman

AP/WIDE WORLD PHOTOS

When Shirley Chisholm ran for the U.S. Congress, she had two strikes against her: She was black and she was a woman. Women had been elected to Congress before, but not many. A black woman had never been elected.

How did a tiny, 90-pound black woman from a poor family get to be a member of Congress? Her grandmother's words help explain it: "The most important thing for you to remember, Shirley, is that your brainpower is going to make the difference in your life." Young Shirley would use that brainpower, and use it well.

Shirley's Childhood

Shirley Chisholm was born Shirley Anita St. Hill in Brooklyn, New York, in 1924. Her parents had come to New York from Barbados, an island in the Caribbean Sea. Even though they worked hard, they were very poor. In the 1920s, black people had a hard time getting good jobs. Her father, Charles St. Hill, had not finished high school, so it was even harder. Shirley's mother earned a small income by sewing at home, and she also took care of Shirley and her two younger sisters. Even though both parents worked, the St. Hills could not earn enough to support themselves and their three daughters.

When Shirley was 3 years old, her parents had to send the three girls to live with their grandmother in Barbados. For the next seven years, the girls lived on a farm, again without much money. Their parents worked to save enough money to bring them back to New York.

What do you think you will learn about Shirley's life in Barbados?

◀ Check-in

Shirley remembered living on her grandmother's farm as "a wonderful life." She and her sisters did chores and worked on the farm. They also picked fresh fruits and vegetables right off the vine and swam every day in the clean, blue water of the Caribbean Sea.

Shirley's parents brought their three daughters back to Brooklyn when she was 10. They had saved enough money to barely support the family. Shirley's father and mother ran a strict household. Her father read three newspapers a day. He gave each child part of a paper to read. They were expected to discuss the articles at dinner. Shirley loved it.

When Shirley was still a young girl, her father took her to political meetings with him. She was often the only child at the meetings. But Shirley didn't mind. Her father wanted her to learn things. He would say, "I want her to learn everything and understand. I want her to ask questions." She learned to listen and to ask questions. It was good training for her future life in politics.

Check-in ▶

College and Early Adult Life

Shirley graduated from high school in 1942 and went to Brooklyn College. She was the first member of her family to attend college. In college, Shirley joined the debate club. She gave many speeches. She spoke intelligently and people listened. One of her professors noticed her ability to influence people with her speeches. Professor Warsoff encouraged her to run for student president. Shirley pointed out that she had very little chance because she was both black and a woman. But Professor Warsoff responded, "Yes, we know that. But you have what it takes." Shirley ran and almost won the election.

What did Shirley learn from her father that would give her the motivation and skills to be a leader later in her life?

After college, Shirley continued to work hard. She became a nursery school teacher. At the same time she earned a master's degree in early childhood education from Columbia University. She worked during the day and went to school at night. During this time, she met and married Conrad Chisholm.

Shirley became active in politics during this period. She joined the local Democratic club in the district where she lived. She dreamed of doing something to help the poor people in her district, and to help women and minorities.

But in the political club, men seemed to control everything. Men decided who would run for political office. They were in charge of the club. Women were never allowed to make decisions. Shirley did not accept this. She formed another group with other minority club members. They worked to register black and Latino voters. Then they helped elect a black candidate.

Chisholm's Political Career

Finally, Shirley decided to run for office herself. "I met with hostility because of my sex from the start of my campaign," she said. People criticized her. They thought she should be home, taking care of her husband. As a black American, Shirley had met with racism throughout her life. But she said, "I have to say that I have met far more discrimination as a woman than as a black in politics." In spite of the critics, Shirley Chisholm was elected to the New York state assembly in 1964. She won by a landslide.[1]

Can you predict the next step in Shirley Chisholm's political career?

◀ **Check-in**

In 1968, Shirley decided to run for the U.S. Congress. She wanted to represent women and minorities in Washington, D.C. Her opponent was a black man who made fun of her. He called her a "little schoolteacher." But Shirley won that race by a landslide, too. She was now one of just eight women in the House of Representatives. She was the only black woman.

AP/WIDE WORLD PHOTOS

In 1972, Shirley set her sights on the highest office in the land —she decided to run for president. She campaigned in 33 states, but did not win her party's nomination. She said: "I think one of my major uses is as an example to the women of our country, to show them that if a woman has ability, stamina, organizational skill, and a knowledge of the issues she can win public office. I can be an instrument for change." And she was.

Shirley Chisholm was elected to Congress seven times in all. With this success, she reached her dream of opening the way for more women and minorities to be elected.

---

1. **landslide:** a large majority vote.

▶ **Final Check-in**
How accurate were your predictions? Did they help you better understand what you read?

After You Read

A. Comprehension Check

1. Name two "handicaps" Shirley Chisholm faced in running for public office.

   _____

2. Tell one way that young Shirley's father helped to prepare her for her future life in politics.

   _____

3. What office was Shirley Chisholm elected to in 1968?

   _____

4. Shirley Chisholm's career might make her a good role model for what two groups of people?

   _____

B. Revisit the Reading Strategy Look back at the predictions you made on page 78. Did this biography include the information you expected? What else did you learn? On the lines below, write three things you learned about Shirley Chisholm's life.

   _____

   _____

   _____

C. Think Beyond the Reading Think about these questions and discuss them with a partner. Answer the questions in writing if you wish.

- Shirley Chisholm had the "brainpower" to become an instrument for change. What other qualities are important in a political leader?
- How can people who don't hold public office help to make changes?

Think About It: Summarize Information

When you summarize, you briefly retell a story, an article, or an event. A summary includes the main idea or topic and the most important details.

How to Write a Summary

1. Identify the topic—what the passage is about.

2. Choose important details that explain the topic.

3. Put the summary into your own words.

A. Look at Summarizing Information

The example below lists important details from the section "Shirley's Childhood" in the biography you just read. The topic, "Shirley Chisholm's Early Childhood," is stated first. The most important details are listed.

Topic: Shirley Chisholm's early childhood
Name: Shirley Anita St. Hill
Date and place of birth: Brooklyn, New York, 1924
Parents: from Barbados, hardworking but poor; when Shirley was age 3 to 10, she and her two sisters lived with grandmother in Barbados; father took her to political meetings, had her read and discuss newspapers when young

Now read the sample summary below.

Sample Summary: Early Years

In 1924 Shirley Anita St. Hill was born in Brooklyn, New York. She would later become Shirley Chisholm. Her family was hardworking but poor. Her parents couldn't support their three children, so Shirley and her two sisters went to live with their grandmother on Barbados. When she was 10, Shirley and her sisters moved back to Brooklyn to live with their parents. Because he recognized the importance of learning, Shirley's father made her read newspapers and discuss them. He also took her to political meetings.

B. Practice

1. Reread the section "College and Early Adult Life." List the most important details from this part of Shirley Chisholm's life.

_____

_____

_____

_____

_____

2. Reread the section "Chisholm's Political Career." List the most important details from her political career.

_____

_____

_____

_____

_____

_____

3. Now write a two-paragraph summary of Shirley Chisholm's life in college and early adulthood and her political career on separate paper. Remember to describe the events in order.

 Talk About It

Tell about someone who made a difference by helping others or by solving a problem. Choose someone you know or a famous person. This list can help you make notes:

- Describe the person.
- Explain what the person did to make a difference.
- Describe the events of that person's life in the order they happened.
- Explain why you think what the person did was important.

Write About It: Write an Autobiography

"Shirley Chisholm: First Black Congresswoman" is a biography written by someone else. An **autobiography** is an account someone writes to describe his or her own life. In this activity you will write an autobiography.

A. Prewriting To organize information about your life, make a rough outline. List events in the order in which they occurred, as in the outline below. The headings are different periods in this person's life: early childhood, elementary school, high school, adulthood.

Write your events on a time line like the one below. Start with the date of your birth. Then list the most important events of each period in your life.

Time line: Sharon K.   My Life

Early childhood	Elementary school	High school	Adulthood

Born July 11, 1980.
When I was 3, parents divorced; went to live with mother.

As a sophomore, won third place in metal-shop contest. Junior year, got my first part-time job—running errands at Parker Auto Parts store. Graduated June 1997.

Not very exciting. When I was 10, broke my arm falling out of a tree. Couldn't do homework for a month!

September 1997 got first full-time job—still at Parker's. This year signed up for auto mechanics school.

B. Writing Write a short autobiography using your time line as a guide.

   a. Write at least one paragraph about each period in your life.
   b. Tell how each period or event was important in your life.

▶ **Save your draft.** At the end of this unit, you will choose one of your drafts to work with further.

Life Skill: Read a Brochure

A **brochure** is a pamphlet or booklet that gives information. Brochures are often about programs or services being offered to the public. Most brochures are only a few pages long. They may use just a few words instead of sentences. You may have to make inferences to understand the message.

Organizations sometimes communicate their ideas through brochures. Sometimes they give important facts about topics such as staying healthy or being a good parent.

Below is a part of a brochure about services offered by St. Joseph Hospital.

Raising Nonviolent Children: What You Can Do

Violent behavior is often learned early in life. Parents can help children learn to deal with situations in nonviolent ways.

For Parenting Information, Join Free Parenting Classes
First and third Tuesday of each month
7:00-8:00 P.M.
St. Joseph Hospital, Room 202
Information: 555-3482
Register by calling the number above
by the Friday before each session.

Tip List
- Don't hit your children.
- Give your children love and attention every day.
- Model nonviolent behavior to show your children how to behave.
- Keep children from seeing violence—at home, in the neighborhood, on TV.

What is the purpose of the tip list?

The tip list gives ideas for helping children learn to be nonviolent.

Practice On separate paper, answer the questions about the brochure sample.

1. What can you infer from the third item on the tip list?
2. Find the important information about how to sign up for the free classes: what? when? where?
3. If you have questions, what can you do?
4. Why do you think people are asked to register in advance?

Lesson 8

LEARNING GOALS

Strategy: Skim
Reading: Read a short story and a voter registration form
Skill: Categorize information
Writing: Write a persuasive letter
Life Skill: Read community announcements

Before You Read

The story "A New Voter in the West End" is about people trying to make a difference by exercising their right to vote. Are you a registered voter? Do you vote in local elections? in national elections? On the lines below, write words or phrases that come to mind when you think about voting.

_____

_____

Preview The Reading

Preview "A New Voter in the West End" by looking at the pictures and **skimming** the story. Read the first sentence in each paragraph. Who do you think the new voter is? Now look over the voter registration form. Do you think it is easy or hard to register to vote?

▶ **Use the Strategy**
You skimmed the story and the voter registration form to get a general impression of them. Now, guided by your general knowledge of what to expect, read to find more specific details.

A New Voter in the West End

Rosa Sanchez is tired of politicians who are all talk and no action. But she has a newfound interest in politics. She recently moved to the West End, and someone from her neighborhood is running for city council. Rosa hopes he will win. She thinks he will give the West End a voice in city government. Yesterday she told her daughter, "Maybe he'll be just another politician. But he's one of us. I think we should give the guy a chance."

Rosa is angry about what she's seen in her new neighborhood. She is worried about safety. She calls the police nearly every week. She wants them to be more visible in the neighborhood. Rosa took her grandchildren to the park last weekend and got angrier. She complained to the others there, "This place is a mess! There's trash and broken glass everywhere. I bet kids on the east side don't have to play in a place like this!"

Today Rosa turned her anger into a plan of action. She wants to hear a new voice on the city council. She wants her new home to be a better place. So she went downtown to register to vote. She's going to vote in the next election.

When Rosa went to register to vote, she was given this form.

You skimmed the form. Do you remember what kind of information it asks for? ◀ **Check-in**

Are you a United States citizen: ❑ By birth ❑ By naturalization[1] ❑ NO IF YOU ANSWERED **NO** DO NOT COMPLETE THIS FORM	**VOTER REGISTRATION APPLICATION** PLEASE TYPE OR PRINT IN CAPITAL LETTERS	

SOCIAL SECURITY NUMBER			SEX	AGE	DATE OF BIRTH			
					Month	Day	Year	

FULL LEGAL NAME (ENTER MAIDEN NAME UNDER PRIOR LEGAL NAME IF NOT PART OF CURRENT LEGAL NAME)

Last Name	First Name	Middle Name	Maiden or other prior legal name

HOME ADDRESS

Street Address	Apartment No.	City	Zip Code	Date moved to this address

PLACE OF BIRTH		CITY & STATE OF PREVIOUS REGISTRATION
City or County	State or Country	

Have you ever been convicted of a felony?[2]	❑ Yes ❑ No	If yes, give date when voting rights were restored.	Month	Day	Year

CHOOSE A PARTY (Check one box only)

❑ Democratic ❑ Liberal
❑ Republican ❑ Right to Life
❑ Conservative ❑ Freedom
❑ Independence ❑ I do not wish to enroll in a party

Registration Statement: I do hereby state that I am a citizen of the United States, a resident of this state qualified under the Constitution to register to vote. I also state that the information above is true and correct to the best of my knowledge. I authorize the cancellation of any previous registration.

Signature or mark	Date
X	/ /

1. naturalization: legal process of becoming a citizen.   **2. felony:** serious crime.

 Final Check-in

Did you know that you have to register in order to vote? Do you think it is easy or hard to register? Why do you think so?

After You Read

A. Comprehension Check

1. Why did Rosa decide to vote?
    (1) She likes the city council as it is now.
    (2) She wants to run for city council.
    (3) She wants a new voice in city government.
    (4) She wants the West End to stay as it is.

2. Rosa is worried that
    (1) the neighborhood is not safe
    (2) air and water are polluted
    (3) the park will close down
    (4) she won't know how to vote

3. The voter registration form asks if you
    (1) are married
    (2) speak and read English
    (3) are a member of a political party
    (4) have been convicted of a felony

4. From reading the registration statement you can infer that a voter must
    (1) be a U.S. citizen
    (2) own a home
    (3) be a high-school graduate
    (4) have a job

5. Put a check next to each item that is on the voter registration application.

    _____ birthdate   _____ birthplace   _____ home address

    _____ employer   _____ sex   _____ name of husband or wife

B. Revisit the Reading Strategy
Think about what you learned as you skimmed the story and voter registration form. How did this help you as you read in more detail?

C. Think Beyond the Reading
Think about these questions and discuss them with a partner. Answer the questions in writing if you wish.

- Do you believe that one vote can make a difference? Why or why not?
- What is the biggest problem in your neighborhood? What would it take to solve it? How could you help?

Think About It: Categorize Information

As you learned in Lesson 2, grouping similar things together is a way to organize information and make it easier to understand and remember. Similar ideas and information are grouped together under general headings called **categories.** Lists and forms are common ways to categorize information. Rosa could organize concerns about her neighborhood into categories.

Safety	Maintenance	Housing
Kids joining gangs	Park a mess	Rising rents
Need more police	Litter on streets	Landlords don't make repairs

Rosa could use the lists to organize her thoughts when she talks to the candidate for city council.

A. Look at Categorizing Information

1. The voter registration application asks for different information. How would you categorize the information below: personal? financial? employment?

SOCIAL SECURITY NUMBER			SEX	AGE	DATE OF BIRTH			
					Month	Day	Year	
FULL LEGAL NAME (ENTER MAIDEN NAME UNDER PRIOR LEGAL NAME IF NOT PART OF CURRENT LEGAL NAME)								
Last Name		First Name			Middle Name		Maiden or other prior legal name	

You were right if you said this section asks for personal information.

2. How would you categorize the information in this section of the form?

_____

Employer	Address
_____	_____
Job Title	Work Phone
_____	_____

This section might be categorized as employment information.

B. Practice Decide how to categorize each section of the voter registration application. Write a category from these choices on the line:

- Eligibility: Right to Vote
- Residence Information
- Sworn Statement and Signature

CHOOSE A PARTY (Check one box only)		**Registration Statement:** I do hereby state that I am a citizen of the United States, a resident of this state qualified under the Constitution to register to vote. I also state that the information above is true and correct to the best of my knowledge. I authorize the cancellation of any previous registration.
❑ Democratic	❑ Liberal	
❑ Republican	❑ Right to Life	
❑ Conservative	❑ Freedom	**Signature or mark** **Date**
❑ Independence	❑ I do not wish to enroll in a party	X / /

1. Category _____

HOME ADDRESS					Date moved to this address
Street Address		Apartment No.	City	Zip Code	
PLACE OF BIRTH			**CITY & STATE OF PREVIOUS REGISTRATION**		
City or County	State or Country				

2. Category _____

Are you a United States citizen:
❑ By birth   ❑ By naturalization[1]   ❑ NO
IF YOU ANSWERED **NO** DO NOT COMPLETE THIS FORM

VOTER REGISTRATION APPLICATION
PLEASE TYPE OR PRINT IN CAPITAL LETTERS

Have you ever been convicted of a felony?[2] ❑ Yes ❑ No	If yes, give date when voting rights were restored.	Month	Day	Year

1. naturalization: legal process of becoming a citizen.   **2. felony:** serious crime.

3. Category _____

 Talk About It

Interview at least three friends about voting. Ask these questions: (1) Is it important to vote? (2) Are you registered? (3) Will you vote in the next local election? Compare your results with others in your group. Discuss these questions: Why do people vote? Why do some people choose not to?

Write About It: Write a Persuasive Letter

"A New Voter in the West End" tells about the improvements Rosa wants for her neighborhood. In this activity you will write a letter to persuade someone to take action on your concerns.

A. Prewriting Read this sample letter that states someone's concerns:

```
March 18, 1998

Ms. Renee Cardoza, General Manager

Dear Ms. Cardoza,
  I think you should know how hard it is to park in the lot
behind the factory. People are often late to work because they
can't find a spot. The early shift takes up all the spots near
the building. On snowy days, the lot is not plowed in the far
sections.
  Plowing more of the lot would help. It would be best if a
spot was assigned to everyone on a rotating basis. Then the
late-shift workers would not always have to walk the farthest.

Sincerely,

Lee Lundy
Machine Operator
```

Choose a topic that you are concerned about. Write a persuasive letter to someone who can do something about your concerns. Use an organizer like the one below to put your ideas in order.

Topic of Letter _____	**To** _____
Problem or Concern _____	Solution(s) _____
_____	_____
_____	_____

B. Writing Write a persuasive letter using your ideas. State your problem in the first sentence of the letter. Then suggest your solution and explain it.

▶ **Save your draft.** At the end of this unit, you will choose one of your drafts to work with further.

Life Skill: Read Community Announcements

Community announcements are found on signs, posters, and in newspapers. They often tell about meetings or special events. Like brochures, they tell only the most important information. Sometimes you must fill in missing words to understand the message.

Read this community announcement.

**Are You Concerned about the West End?
Your Councilman Wants to Hear from You**

Raymond Cruz, City Councilman
Speaking at
Grady Memorial Community Church
Sunday, October 6, 1:00 P.M.

Air your concerns during
the question and answer period.
This is your chance to be heard!

Sponsored by Citizens for Better Government

What is the announcement about? Find the place and time.

The announcement tells about a speech by a city councilman. It is at the Grady Memorial Community Church at 1:00 P.M. on October 6.

Practice Read the announcement and answer the questions on separate paper.

**Hillsboro City School Board
Business Meeting**

September 21, 7:30 P.M.   Ford Middle School

Topics for Discussion:

♦ Code of Conduct and related
  School Board policy changes

♦ Appointment of new representative
  to Parent Advisory Council

Delayed broadcast of meeting can be seen on Channel 2,
Sept. 22 at 7:00 P.M.

---

1. Get the basic facts. What is happening? When and where?
2. What kind of School Board policy changes will be discussed?
3. If you miss the meeting, how can you find out what happened?

Lesson 9

LEARNING GOALS

Strategy: Use your prior knowledge
Reading: Read letters to the editor
Skill: Identify facts and opinions
Writing: Write a letter to the editor
Life Skill: Read bar graphs

Before You Read

People write letters to the editor to tell how they feel about some issue or event. They hope the newspaper will print their letter so the public can read their opinion.

The readings in this lesson are letters to the editor of a local newspaper. Several people have written to give their opinion about volunteers in their public schools. The knowledge you already have about public schools will help you to understand the letters. Use your **prior knowledge** now. On the lines below, write two ways that volunteers helped or could have helped in your schools.

_____

_____

Preview the Reading

To preview the reading selection, look at the picture. Then look over the letters to the editor and see who wrote them. How do you think these different people will feel about volunteers in the public schools? Then skim the bar graphs to see the kind of information they provide.

Think about what you know about elementary schools today. How would you feel about the situation described in these letters?

Letters to the Editor: Volunteers in Schools

LETTERS TO THE EDITOR

Dear Editor:

I am writing to thank the many classroom volunteers at Taylor Elementary School who gave their time and talents to help our children. This year, 45 volunteers worked over 1200 hours at Taylor Elementary.

They worked in classrooms and in the media center. They also helped in the after-school program. They read stories to children and helped with reading, spelling, and math. To put it simply, the volunteers gave kids the individual attention they needed to succeed. And we really needed the volunteers.

Over the last two years, our school enrollment has grown by 20 percent. That meant an average of five more children in every classroom. Because of funding cuts, we couldn't hire more teachers. We also had to cut back hours for teacher's aides. Last year, it was hard for our teachers and aides to find time to work with children who needed individual help. This year, volunteers worked with these children one-to-one and in small groups to keep them from falling behind.

Volunteers have contributed greatly to successful school experiences for many of our students. Volunteers like these should be part of every school.

Gwen Martinez, Principal
Taylor Elementary School

Read these reactions to the principal's letter. Use what you know about children, parents, and teachers to understand the different points of view in these letters.

◀ Check-in

Who do you agree with? Use what you know about schools to decide.

◀ Check-in

LETTERS TO THE EDITOR

Dear Editor:

This is in regard to Mrs. Martinez's letter of June 28. I agree with Mrs. Martinez that the volunteers at Taylor have been a big help. They really care about the kids. But I care too. I'm a teacher's aide, and I had my job cut this year from 20 to 15 hours a week. Most of the other aides got cut back too.

I don't think the school should try to get work for free. It's not fair to trained classroom aides. We work with the kids every day, and we do a good job. Sometimes the volunteers help me out and I think they are great, but they shouldn't take our place. The schools should use trained, paid workers, instead of asking for more volunteers.

LaVonne Brown, Teacher's Aide
Taylor Elementary School

Dear Editor:

I am the parent of a 4-year-old child who will go to Taylor Elementary next year. My older daughter needed special help with reading when she was in elementary school. If my preschooler needs help in a year or two, I hope a real teacher will be available. We should give our children the best that we have.

I am glad that the volunteers "stepped up to the plate." The classes were crowded, and the teachers couldn't do it all. But I feel that the best answer is not more volunteers. It's more teachers. Volunteers are a great help on field trips. But I think schools should have trained teachers helping children with reading and math. That's why we pay our taxes.

Brian Szymanski, Parent

Why Volunteers Are Needed

The following graphs appeared in the same newspaper that printed the letters to the editor you just read. The first graph shows the increase in enrollment at Taylor Elementary over the past two years. Population in the Taylor neighborhood had grown rapidly. In two years, average class size went from 25 students per class to 30 students per class. As a result, the school asked for volunteers to help teachers in the classrooms. Read the second graph to see how people responded to the call for volunteers.

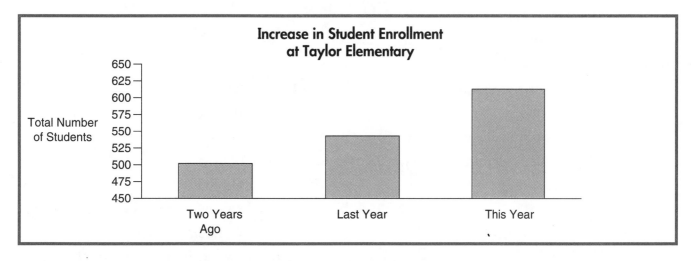

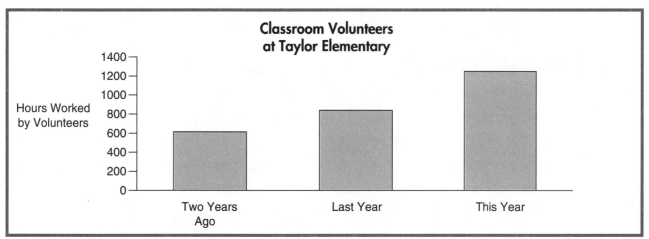

The graph shows that the time given by classroom volunteers at Taylor Elementary has grown by more than 100 percent in the last two years.

▶ **Final Check-in**

Do you think it is important for people to volunteer in community services and organizations? Why or why not?

After You Read

A. Comprehension Check

1. Ms. Martinez mainly writes to
   (1) complain about the volunteers
   (2) thank the volunteers
   (3) praise the children and teachers
   (4) complain about crowded classrooms

2. What does LaVonne Brown think?
   (1) The schools should use paid workers.
   (2) The schools should get more volunteers.
   (3) The volunteers are not helpful.
   (4) The aides should work fewer hours.

3. Brian Szymanski wants the schools to
   (1) recruit more volunteers
   (2) hire more paid aides in the classroom
   (3) train volunteers to work with children
   (4) have trained teachers to help children

4. The second graph on page 99 shows
   (1) different ways volunteers have helped
   (2) the growth in the number of volunteers
   (3) the growth in the number of hours volunteers worked
   (4) the growth in the number of students per class

B. Revisit the Reading Strategy

Use what you know about today's schools to suggest ways to help children learn. Which of the ideas below would be most helpful? Write 1, 2, and 3, next to your top three choices.

_____ more teachers and smaller classes

_____ more help from parents

_____ more work on reading

_____ stricter rules and better behavior

_____ tutors for special help

_____ longer school days and school year

_____ more work on math

_____ more homework

C. Think Beyond the Reading

Think about these questions and discuss them with a partner. Answer the questions in writing if you wish.

- What changes would you suggest to improve public schools?
- Who is responsible for education? Teachers? Parents? All citizens? What can each group contribute?

Think About It: Identify Facts and Opinions

Letters to the editor contain many opinions. They may also contain facts that support the opinions. Sometimes opinions are stated as if they are facts. It is important for you to be able to identify the difference between **facts** and **opinions,** especially if you are making decisions based on them.

As you learned in Lesson 6, a **fact** is a statement that can be shown to be real or actual. It can be seen, heard, or felt; looked up in a reliable source; or supported scientifically. The example below is a fact that can be supported by observation.

>Volunteers worked with children at Taylor Elementary School.

An **opinion** is a statement that hasn't been proven. An opinion states a person's belief or suggests what might or should happen. Statements of opinion sometimes use words like *think, believe, feel, should,* and *agree.* The opinion below suggests something that *should* happen.

>We need more volunteers in the classroom.

A. Look at Identifying Facts and Opinions

1. Read the statement below from Ms. Martinez's letter. Is it an opinion or a fact? How can you tell?

>▶ Volunteers like these should be part of every school.

The statement is an opinion. The word *should* tells you that Ms. Martinez is stating her belief, not a fact.

2. Which of the following statements is a fact? Which is an opinion?

>▶ I don't think the school should try to get work for free.

>▶ This year at Taylor Elementary, 45 volunteers worked over 1,200 hours at our school.

The first sentence is an opinion. Ms. Brown uses the words *think* and *should.* The next sentence is a fact. The school has records to support it.

B. Practice Find the facts and opinions in the statements below. On the line next to each statement, write **F** for **Fact** or **O** for **Opinion.**

_____ 1. I agree with Ms. Martinez that the volunteers at Taylor have been a big help.

_____ 2. Over the last two years, enrollment at Taylor Elementary grew by 20 percent.

_____ 3. Population in the Taylor neighborhood is growing.

_____ 4. We should give our children the best that we have.

_____ 5. The schools should use trained, paid workers, instead of asking for more volunteers.

_____ 6. I had my hours cut this year from 20 to 15 hours a week.

_____ 7. I feel that the best answer is not more volunteers.

_____ 8. The schools should have only trained teachers helping children with reading and math.

_____ 9. It's not fair to us.

_____ 10. They read stories to children and helped with reading, spelling, and math.

▶ **Talk About It**

When people discuss topics that have many sides, both facts and opinions are voiced. You need to learn how to tell whether people are stating facts or opinions. Discuss this question:
• What kinds of activities should volunteers help with in schools?

Make notes of the important points people make. Notice any facts that are used to support opinions.

Write About It: Write a Letter to the Editor

You have read the letters about school volunteers. Now write your own letter to the editor. Choose a problem in your own community.

A. **Prewriting** Read this sample letter to the editor. Notice that the writer states what he wants done—his solution. He also gives reasons, both facts and opinions, for why he wants it done.

LETTERS TO THE EDITOR

Dear Editor:

I am writing because we need more police patrols in the Westwood section of our city.

Drivers are speeding in this section and endangering our children. They often park wherever they want and block driveways. This violates our rights.

We need to find a way to give us more police patrols and return peace to our neighborhood. Readers who agree can call me at 555-1122. Together we can form a task force. We can make a difference!

Roberto DeAngelo
Westwood

Now make notes for the letter you want to write.

Problem: _____

My solution: _____

My reasons: _____

_____

_____

_____

B. **Writing** Now write your letter to the editor.

1. Begin by stating the problem and your solution.
2. Then state your reasons, both facts and opinions.
3. End your letter with a convincing statement or a call to action.

▶ **Save your draft.** At the end of this unit, you will choose one of your drafts to work with further.

Life Skill: A Closer Look at a Bar Graph

In Lesson 1, you saw how information can be presented in a circle graph. The information on page 99 in this lesson was displayed in a different kind of graph—a bar graph. To understand a bar graph, first read the title to see what it is about. Then read the labels to see what the numbers and bars stand for.

The bar graph on this page shows information about how Americans volunteer their time.

A. Practice Look at the bar graph. Read the title and labels carefully. Then answer the questions.

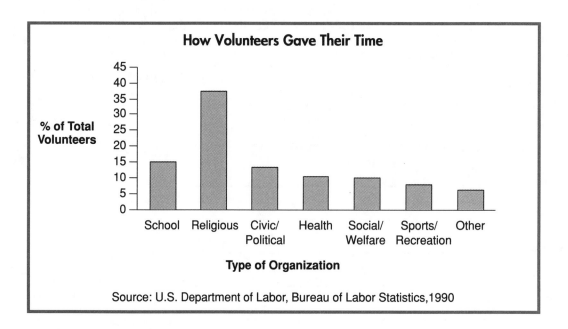

How Volunteers Gave Their Time

% of Total Volunteers

Type of Organization

School   Religious   Civic/Political   Health   Social/Welfare   Sports/Recreation   Other

Source: U.S. Department of Labor, Bureau of Labor Statistics, 1990

1. What kind of organization had the most volunteers? _____

2. What percent of volunteers gave their time to schools? _____

People who read the same graph may interpret it differently. For example, the graph on this page can be read in more than one way. One person might feel that it shows that people volunteer in many ways to help others in their communities. Another person might feel that the graph mainly shows that more people volunteer in religious organizations than in any other area.

The graph on this page is about children's reading skills. It compares the reading scores of children who read for fun every day with the scores of children who seldom read for fun. The reading scores are measured by a national test of reading skills. Notice that there are two bars for each age shown. This is called a double bar graph. The key beside the graph tells you what the two bars stand for.

B. Practice Read the title of the graph, the labels, and the key. Answer the questions.

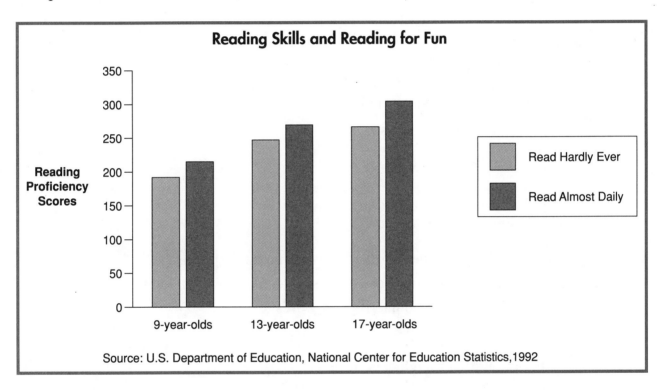

3. Find the bar that stands for 9-year-olds who read for fun daily. About what score did they get on the test? _____

4. What was the score for 9-year-olds who hardly ever read? _____

5. Look at both bars for 13-year-olds. Then look at both bars for 17-year-olds. What do they tell you about students who read for fun almost daily?

_____

6. In your opinion, what is the main idea of the graph? _____

_____

Writing Skills Mini-Lesson:
More on Making Subjects and Verbs Agree

Verbs must agree with their subjects. Pay particular attention to this rule when you write in the **present tense.** Watch out for these tricky situations.

1. **Compound subjects.** You can join two singular subjects with the word *and* to make a compound subject. A compound subject is plural, so don't add *s* to a present tense verb. For the verb *to be,* use *are.*

   Singular
   Subject Verb

   Alonso wants to join the Parent Teacher Association.

   Compound
   Subject   Verb

   Alonso and Leticia want to join the PTA.

   Singular
   Subject Verb

   My wife is a member of the PTA.

   Compound
   Subject   Verb

   My wife and I are members of the PTA.

2. **Interrupting words.** Sometimes a group of words comes between the subject and the verb. To choose the correct present tense verb form, look back to the subject and ignore the interrupting words.

   Singular
   Subject   Verb

   The **teacher** of our twin daughters **is** new.

   Plural
   Subject   Verb

   Parents who are active in the school **help** all the children.

Practice Copy each sentence, choosing the correct form of the verb.
Underline the subject.

1. (am, are) My wife and I _____ the parents of twin daughters.
2. (goes, go) Our daughters and their best friend _____ to Ray School.
3. (is, are) Selena and Cristina _____ in the second grade.
4. (is, are) The association of parents and teachers _____ active at Ray.
5. (works, work) The teachers at Ray School _____ well with the parents.
6. (needs, need) Every parent of young children _____ to join the PTA.

Unit 3 Review

Reading Review

Small Acts

Mark felt that it was time for him to take part in his community, so he went to the neighborhood meeting after work. The area's city councilwoman was leading a discussion about how the quality of life was on the decline. The neighborhood faced many problems.

Mark looked at the charts taped to the walls. There were charts for parking problems, crime, and for problems in vacant buildings. Information about the problems was written on the charts. Mark read from the charts. "Squatters pose fire hazards in 123 vacant buildings." "Police patrols cut back." "Illegal parking up 20%." People were supposed to suggest solutions to the councilwoman.

It was too much for Mark. "The problems are too big," he thought. He turned to the man next to him and said, "I think this is a waste of my time. Nothing I could do would make a difference here."

Mark thought some more on his way to the bus stop. "People should just take care of themselves," he decided. "That's enough to do. I can't take on all the problems of the world."

As he neared the bus stop, Mark saw a woman carrying a grocery bag and a baby. She was trying to unlock her car, but she didn't have a free hand. As Mark got closer, her other child, a little boy, suddenly darted into the street. The woman tried to reach for him, but as she moved, her bag shifted and groceries started to fall out. Mark ran to take the boy's arm and led him back to his mother. "Hold on there, buddy," he said. "You gotta stay with Mom." Then he picked up the stray groceries while the woman smiled in relief. "Thanks!" she said. "You've got great timing!"

"Just being neighborly," Mark said. As he rode home, he glanced at the graffiti on the walls of the bus. Someone had scribbled, "Small acts of kindness add up." Mark smiled and thought, "Maybe that's a good place to start."

Answer the questions.

1. This story is about
   (1) realizing that individuals can make a difference
   (2) running a neighborhood meeting
   (3) problems in our country
   (4) solving problems through group action

2. Number the four statements below in the correct order to summarize the story.
   _____ **a.** On his way home, Mark rescued a little boy who had run into the street.
   _____ **b.** Mark went to a meeting about neighborhood problems.
   _____ **c.** He realized that it was important for each person to help make life better.
   _____ **d.** He decided he couldn't do anything to make life better in his neighborhood.

3. Find the facts and opinions in the statements below. On the line next to each statement, write **F** for **Fact** or **O** for **Opinion**.
   _____ **a.** I think this is a waste of my time.   _____ **d.** Police patrols have been cut back.
   _____ **b.** The problems are too big.   _____ **e.** Illegal parking is up 20%.
   _____ **c.** People should just take care of   _____ **f.** You've got great timing!
   themselves.

Writing Process

In Unit 3, you wrote three first drafts. Choose the piece that you would like to work with further. You will revise, edit, and make a final copy of this draft.
   _____ your short autobiography based on a time line (page 86)
   _____ your persuasive letter to convince someone to take action (page 94)
   _____ your letter to the editor about a problem in your community (page 103)

Find the first draft you chose. Then turn to page 160 in this book. Follow steps 3, 4, and 5 in the Writing Process to create a final draft.

As you revise, check your draft for these specific points:
Autobiography: Have you included the important events in your life?
Persuasive letter: Be sure you suggested some action to take.
Letter to the editor: Was your reason for writing clearly stated?

Unit 4 Many Cultures

Unless you are a Native American, either you or someone related to you came to the United States from another country. Elements of that country's way of life may have become part of the culture of the United States. In this way, the United States has gradually developed the varied culture we know today. And every year, more people add parts of their own backgrounds to the vast patchwork quilt that is the culture of the United States. What cultural background did your family bring to this country? What elements of that culture have become part of the heritage of the United States?

▶ **Be an Active Reader**

As you read the selections in this unit
- Put a question mark (?) by things you do not understand.
- <u>Underline</u> words you do not know. Try to use context clues to figure them out.

After you read each selection in this unit
- Reread sections you marked with a question mark (?). If they still do not make sense, discuss them with a partner or your instructor.
- Look at words you <u>underlined</u>. Discuss any words you still don't understand with a partner or your instructor, or look them up in a dictionary.

Lesson 10

LEARNING GOALS

Strategy: Imagine
Reading: Read fables
Skill: Compare and contrast
Writing: Write a fable
Life Skill: Read a map

Before You Read

The four short readings in this lesson are fables. Fables are tales that have been told for hundreds of years by people of many cultures. They teach important lessons about life, often called "morals." Many fables, including the fables in this lesson, are about animals that talk and act like humans. Fables are shared by people all over the world.

To understand the fables, you will have to use your imagination. **Imagine** yourself as an eagle, a rabbit, a turtle, or some other animal. What do you look like? How do you feel? Where do you live? What are you best known for? Write the name of your animal and your answers on the lines below.

_____

_____

_____

_____

Preview the Reading

To preview the four fables, read their titles and look at the pictures. What animals are the stories about? What do you know about these animals? Where do they live? How do they get from one place to another? Try to predict what might happen in the fables.

▶ **Use the Strategy**

As you read the four fables, try to imagine what is happening and how the animals look and feel. The first fable comes from Russia.

The Eagle and the Spider

An eagle had soared above the clouds to the highest peak of a mountain range, and perching upon an old tree, admired the view below. It seemed as though the whole world could be seen from that height.

"Heaven be praised," said the eagle, "for giving me such powers of flight, that there is no mountain too high for me to reach. I am now looking down upon the beauties of the world from a point which no other living creature has ever reached!"

"What a boaster you are," said a spider from a nearby branch. "Where I am sitting isn't so far below you, is it, friend eagle?"

The eagle glanced upward. True enough, the spider was busily spinning its web from a branch above his head.

"However did you reach this height?" asked the eagle. "Weak and wingless, as you are, how did you ever crawl way up here?"

"Why, I fastened myself onto you," returned the spider. "You yourself brought me from down below hanging onto your tail feathers. But now that I am so high up in the world I can get along very well by myself, without your help. So you needn't put on any airs with me. For I want to tell you that—"

At this moment a sudden gust of wind swept by, and brushed the spider, web and all, back down again into the valley from which it had come.

Check-in ▶ Did you imagine the spider and the eagle as you read? How do you think the spider felt before he fell? After he fell?

The next two fables come from an ancient Greek storyteller called Aesop (EE sop). Aesop's fables always end with a moral, a lesson about life. As you read, imagine how the animals feel as they learn the lessons.

The Tortoise and the Eagle

A tortoise was dissatisfied with his lowly life, when he saw so many of the birds, his neighbors, playing about in the clouds. He thought that if he could once get up into the air, he could soar with the best of them. So he called one day upon an eagle and offered him all the treasures of the ocean if he would teach him to fly. The eagle would have refused, because he thought the idea was not only absurd, but impossible. But the tortoise pleaded with him, and he finally agreed to do for him the best he could.

The eagle took the tortoise up to a great height in the air and let him go. "Now then!" cried the eagle. But the tortoise, before he could say a word, fell straight down upon a rock, and was dashed to pieces.

Moral: Pride comes before a fall.

The Hare and the Tortoise

A hare made fun of a tortoise because of his slow pace. But the tortoise laughed and said that he would run against the hare and beat her any day she would name. "Come on," said the hare, "you shall soon see what my feet are made of." So it was agreed that they would start at once. The tortoise went off, jogging along at his usual steady pace without a moment's stopping. The hare treated the whole matter very lightly. She said she would first take a little nap and would soon catch up with the tortoise and pass him by. Meanwhile, the tortoise plodded on and the hare overslept, so that when she arrived at the goal, she saw that the tortoise had got there before her.

Moral: Slow and steady wins the race.

Check-in ▶ Imagine what kind of person the hare would be if she were human. Describe both the hare and the tortoise as if they were people.

The fable below comes from a Native American culture. As you read it, picture the pigeon-hawk's journey.

The Pigeon-Hawk[1] and the Tortoise

The pigeon-hawk challenged the tortoise to a race. The tortoise would not accept the challenge unless the hawk would agree to race several days' journey. The hawk very quickly agreed, and they immediately set out. The tortoise knew that to win the race he would have to work very hard. So he went down into the earth and, digging in a straight line, stopped for nothing. The hawk, on the other hand, knowing that he could easily win, kept carelessly flying this way and that in the air. He stopped to visit one friend and then another. He lost so much time that when he came in sight of the winning point, the tortoise had just come up out of the earth and gained the prize.

---

1. pigeon-hawk: a small falcon, a bird of prey.

► **Final Check-in**

How do you imagine the hawk felt when he challenged the tortoise?
How did he feel when he saw that the tortoise would win?

After You Read

A. Comprehension Check

1. In the first fable, the eagle and the spider
   (1) become good friends
   (2) brag about their abilities
   (3) fall down to the ground
   (4) learn to help each other

2. What lesson can we learn from the first two fables?
   (1) Work hard.
   (2) Don't be selfish.
   (3) Save for a rainy day.
   (4) Don't be too proud.

3. The pigeon-hawk lost because
   (1) digging is faster than flying
   (2) he didn't try hard enough
   (3) he hurt his wing
   (4) his friends wouldn't help him

4. In each of the last two fables, the tortoise won because he
   (1) was a steady worker
   (2) didn't play by the rules
   (3) got a head start
   (4) could move faster

B. Revisit the Reading Strategy
Imagine yourself as the hare or the pigeon-hawk in the last two fables. How would you feel at the end of the race? Check all the words that describe your feelings.

_____ angry   _____ proud   _____ embarrassed

_____ foolish   _____ excited   _____ disappointed

C. Think Beyond the Reading
Think about these questions and discuss them with a partner. Answer the questions in writing if you wish.

- Important lessons about life may be learned from fables. What are the morals of these stories? Try to explain them in your own words.

- How do you best learn about life? Do you learn by listening to others' stories and advice, or through your own experiences, or both?

Think About It: Compare and Contrast

To understand the actions, feelings, and ideas of people from other cultures, we often compare and contrast them with our own. To **compare,** we see how things are alike or similar. To **contrast,** we notice how they are different.

You can also compare and contrast to understand people and ideas in a passage. For example, you might compare the first two fables based on their titles: "The Eagle and the Spider" and "The Tortoise and the Eagle."

Compare (How alike?)	Contrast (How different?)
• Each has two animals.	• One has a spider, and
• Each has an eagle.	the other has a tortoise.

A. Look at Compare and Contrast

The endings of the first two fables are compared and contrasted below:

▶ . . . a sudden gust of wind swept by, and brushed the spider, web and all, back down again into the valley from which it had come.

▶ . . . the tortoise, before he could say a word, fell straight down upon a rock, and was dashed to pieces.

Compare	Contrast
• Both animals fell to earth.	• The tortoise was killed; the spider was swept down but not killed.

Read the passage below. How did the pigeon-hawk and the tortoise run the race differently?

▶ The tortoise . . . went down into the earth and, digging in a straight line, stopped for nothing. The hawk, . . . knowing that he could easily win, kept carelessly flying this way and that . . .

You were right if you said

• the tortoise traveled underground; the pigeon-hawk flew
• the tortoise went in a straight line; the pigeon-hawk went "this way and that"

B. Practice Answer the questions. Look back at the fables to check details. You may use charts like the ones on page 116 to organize your ideas.

1. Compare the two fables "The Eagle and the Spider" and "The Tortoise and the Eagle." Each is about an eagle and another animal. Name another important way that they are similar.

   _____

2. Think about the pigeon-hawk and the hare in the last two fables. Name one difference in their actions. Name one way their actions are similar.

   Different: _____

   Similar: _____

3. "The Hare and the Tortoise" and "The Pigeon-Hawk and the Tortoise" are stories from different cultures. The first is Greek and the second is Native American, but they are similar. Name two ways they are alike.

   _____   _____

4. Compare and contrast the two fables "The Tortoise and the Eagle" and "The Pigeon-Hawk and the Tortoise." Name one way they are similar and one way they are different.

   Similar: _____

   Different: _____

5. The fables you read came from very different parts of the world. What does this fact suggest about these different cultures? How are they similar?

   _____

▶ **Talk About It**

Tell a partner a story about an experience or event in your life that taught you or someone else a lesson.

• Tell the story in the order in which events happened. Give details.

• Tell why the experience was important and what you learned from it.

Compare your story with your partner's story and discuss the lessons you each learned.

Write About It: Write a Fable

In this lesson you read fables from around the world. Now write your own fable. Use animals as characters in your fable. Write about something that taught them a lesson.

A. Prewriting Look at the sample story map below. The story map begins with a statement of the original event or problem. Then it briefly describes a chain of events in order. Last, it states the lesson learned from the story.

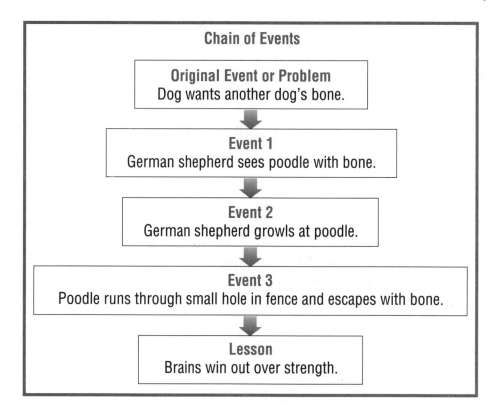

Chain of Events

> **Original Event or Problem**
> Dog wants another dog's bone.

> **Event 1**
> German shepherd sees poodle with bone.

> **Event 2**
> German shepherd growls at poodle.

> **Event 3**
> Poodle runs through small hole in fence and escapes with bone.

> **Lesson**
> Brains win out over strength.

Make your own story map to start your fable. Have three or more events in your chain of events.

B. Writing Write a story, using the chain of events from your story map.

- Write the events in the order in which they happened.
- Give descriptive details.
- End with the lesson the animal characters learned.

▶ **Save your draft.** At the end of this unit, you will choose one of your drafts to work with further.

Life Skill: Read a Map

The fables in this lesson came from different parts of the world. You can see where these fables came from by looking at a map.

A **map** is a representation of an area. The world map on this page shows the continents and major bodies of water on the earth. A continent is a huge land mass that usually includes several countries. Names of continents are in the largest letters. The map gives the names of the oceans and some countries. Directions are shown on the "compass" in the corner of the map: *N* (north) at the top of the map, *S* for south, *E* for east, and *W* for west.

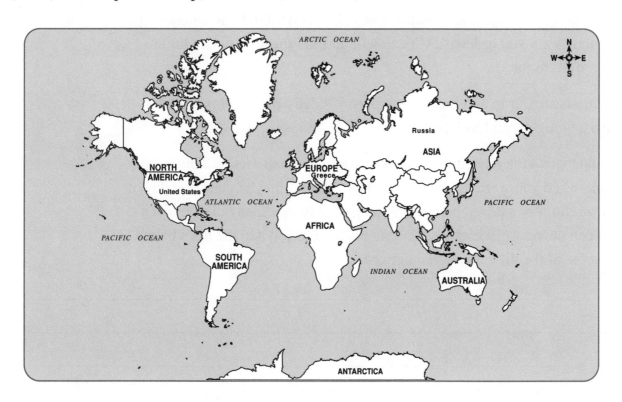

Practice Answer the questions on separate paper.

1. Name the seven continents.
2. Greece is on what continent?
3. What ocean is north of Russia?
4. What ocean lies to the east of the United States?
5. What continent is north of Africa?
6. What continent is east of the Indian Ocean?

Lesson 11

LEARNING GOALS

Strategy: Use your prior experience
Reading: Read a diary entry
Skill: Make inferences
Writing: Write a diary entry
Life Skill: Read a schedule

Before You Read

The reading in this lesson is a diary entry. It was written by Raimonda Kopelnitsky, a young Jewish woman who left the former Soviet Union and moved to the U.S.

A diary is similar to a journal. It is a person's daily record of personal events, thoughts, and feelings.

To understand the reading, you can use your **prior experience.** Think about a time when you were a beginner or a newcomer—maybe your first day at a new school or a new job. At first, you probably saw many differences between the new place and your former school or job. On the lines below, list some of the differences you noticed.

_____

_____

_____

Preview the Reading

Before you read, preview the diary entry. Look at the pictures. Try to predict what you will learn from this diary.

▶ Use the Strategy

Remember how it felt to be a beginner or a newcomer as you read Raimonda Kopelnitsky's account of being a newcomer in the U.S.

No Words to Say Good-bye

CORBIS/BETTMANN

December 16, 1990

Hi, dear Kitty,

Today Mama and I went to Manhattan.[1] We met Rose, the woman who first took us to the synagogue[2] when we were still living in the hotel. We hadn't heard from her in a while. We walked in the city and saw the windows of stores where dolls move. Then we went to Rockefeller Center. There was a big green tree and it was beautiful. There was also an orchestra of five hundred people that was playing American Christmas songs.

In that moment I was trying to remember the Soviet New Year. All the members of our family and our closest friends gathered together. We made a big table of food. We ate

---

1. **Manhattan:** a part of New York City.
2. **synagogue:** a Jewish place of worship.

from ten till six in the morning. We had a big green tree[3] that would stick its top to the ceiling. Then at midnight our president would show up on TV and tell about the year, its problems and his wishes for the next year. Then the Soviet hymn would play and everyone would stand up to meet the New Year. After that, the TV was on the whole night with New Year's jokes, concerts, and music. I knew all those songs, the music, the people. I stopped remembering.

Did your own holiday experiences help you to picture Raimonda's description of her New Year's celebration?

◄ **Check-in**

Now, I don't know these American Christmas songs that sound so beautiful, nor these people. It's a pity, or maybe not. There'll be a day when I forget my past, and music from the past, and people. There'll be a day when I know these American songs and these people. At least both of these cultures will always celebrate New Year's with me. There will always be a new year, and it will always be celebrated. So even if I don't know American songs or will someday forget Russian songs, the sentiments[4] will still mean the same thing.

Raimonda

3. **background note:** In the former Soviet Union, under Communism, there was no Christmas celebration. But New Year's was celebrated with a holiday tree.
4. **sentiments:** the emotional meaning of a passage; the feelings behind the words.

▶ **Final Check-in**
Did it help to recall your own experience to understand Raimonda's thoughts? How did she feel about leaving her own culture?

After You Read

A. Comprehension Check

  1. Name two things Raimonda and her mother saw when they visited Manhattan.

  _____

  _____

  2. The sights and songs of the American Christmas season brought

  back Raimonda's memories of the Soviet celebration of _____

  3. List three things that Raimonda remembered about the Soviet celebration.

  _____

  _____

  _____

  4. Although the American celebration seemed strange to her, Raimonda

  predicted that one day _____

  5. What does Raimonda think is the same about the American and Russian

  songs? _____

B. Revisit the Reading Strategy On page 120, you listed differences you
felt when you were a newcomer or a beginner. How did you learn about
your new surroundings and fit in? Check the strategies that you used.

  _____ watched other people   _____ read information provided for newcomers
  _____ asked for help   _____ followed printed directions
  _____ found a "buddy"   _____ listened to advice

  other strategies _____

C. Think Beyond the Reading Think about these questions and discuss them
with a partner. Answer the questions in writing if you wish.

  • What experiences have you had with other cultures?
  • What other cultures have celebrations similar to holidays in the United States?
  • What other cultures have celebrations different from those in the United States?

Think About It: Make Inferences

Making inferences is a skill you use every day. You learned in Lesson 4 that when you infer, you use clues to figure out something that isn't actually stated. For instance, you can infer people's feelings and the reasons behind their actions by watching and listening to them. Imagine the following scene in a hospital:

> A man and woman, carrying a bouquet of flowers, are pointing to signs on the wall and looking puzzled. They are speaking Spanish excitedly.

You may not know the people or their language. But you can use your experience and the clues in their actions to infer that they are confused and may need help.

A. Look at Making Inferences

When you read, you can use clues to fill in the missing pieces. For example, Raimonda writes to "Kitty," but she does not explain who Kitty is. Since a diary is a personal record not read by others, you might infer that Kitty is the name Raimonda has given to her diary. Or perhaps Kitty is an imaginary friend.

1. Here's another example. Use the clues below to figure out who Rose is.

    > ▶ We met Rose, the woman who first took us to the synagogue when we were still living in the hotel. We hadn't heard from her in a while.

    You might infer that Rose is an American, someone from the Soviet Union who has been in the U.S. longer than Raimonda and her family. The diary suggests that Rose helped them learn about the U.S.

2. Now use your knowledge of human nature to infer what Raimonda was feeling in the next passage. Why do you think she stopped remembering?

    > ▶ All the members of our family and our closest friends gathered together. . . . I knew all those songs, the music, the people. I stopped remembering.

    You might infer that her memories made her homesick. Maybe she stopped remembering because she was missing people and feeling sad.

B. Practice Read the passages and infer answers to the questions.

1. ▶ We walked in the city and saw the windows of stores where dolls move.

   a. Why do you think Raimonda noticed the dolls?

   _____

   b. What do you think the dolls were?

   _____

2. ▶ Then we went to Rockefeller Center. There was a big green tree
   and it was beautiful.

   What do you think the big green tree was? _____

3. ▶ . . . both of these cultures will always celebrate New Year's with me.
   There will always be a new year, and it will always be celebrated. So even
   if I don't know American songs or will someday forget Russian songs,
   the sentiments will still mean the same thing.

   Based on this passage, does Raimonda think the American and
   Soviet celebrations are similar in important ways, or very different?
   Why do you think so?

   _____

   _____

▶ **Talk About It**
Talk with a partner or a small group about the problems faced
by people who come from other countries to live in the U.S.
Discuss these questions.
- Why do people make such a major move? What are some possible
  reasons?
- What problems do newcomers face?
- What do they need to learn?
- How can people already living in the U.S. help them?

Write About It: Write a Diary Entry

In this lesson, you read an entry from the diary of a young Russian woman. She described her feelings about an important event in her life: moving to the United States. Now write your own diary entry about an experience in your life.

A. **Prewriting** Choose a big event in your life such as a move, a new job, the birth of a child, or a big project. Usually people don't make detailed plans before writing in a diary. But this time it may help to make some notes. First, think about your topic. Then, on separate paper, make your own lists in the pattern shown below. In one list write details about the event. In the other list write your feelings about the event.

Event My son's birth	
What Happened	**My Feelings**
David born 1-5-96	excited and proud
our first child	glad for the good times
healthy and strong, a good boy	lucky and grateful
long labor	tired and in pain
my whole family came to see him in the hospital	happy to show him to the family

B. **Writing** Write a diary entry. Pretend you are writing on the day of the event, or write about your memory of it, as in the example.

- Write the date at the top of the page. Then begin your entry with "Dear Diary" or give your diary a name, as Raimonda did.
- Be sure your entry includes details about the event and how you felt.

▶ **Save your draft.** At the end of this unit, you will choose one of your drafts to work with further.

Life Skill: Read a Schedule

A **schedule** is a chart that lists information about events or services. To find information on a schedule, read down the column on the left until you find the row you want. Then read across the row to find times and other information.

People from different cultures might use a schedule like the one on this page to sign up for English classes.

Northeast Community Center
Schedule of Adult Education Classes

ABE = Adult Basic Education
GED = General Educational Development
ESL = English as a Second Language

Days	Times	Room	Instructor
ABE Classes			
Mon. & Wed.	2:30 P.M.– 4:30 P.M.	101A	M. Danner
Tues. & Thurs.	9:00 A.M.– 11:00 A.M.	101A	S. Burnett
	7:00 P.M.– 9:00 P.M.	105	R. Cohen
GED Classes			
Mon. & Wed.	9:00 A.M.– 11:00 A.M.	201A	M. Danner
Tues. & Thurs.	2:30 P.M.– 4:30 P.M.	201A	R. Cohen
	7:00 P.M.– 9:00 P.M.	205	J. Mundo
ESL Classes			
Mon. & Wed.	9:00 A.M.– 11:00 A.M.	102	T. Feng
Tues. & Thurs.	7:00 P.M.– 9:00 P.M.	102	H. Ruiz
Night High School			
Mon. – Thurs.	6:30 P.M.– 9:00 P.M.	101B	A. Pirelli

Practice Read the schedule. Then answer these questions on separate paper.

1. When and where are the Night High School classes held?
2. When can a person learn English in the evening?
3. Who teaches the morning ESL classes? The evening classes?
4. If you work during the day, when and where can you take an ABE class?
5. Who teaches the morning GED classes? Where do they meet?

Lesson 12

LEARNING GOALS

Strategy: Set a purpose
Reading: Read an essay
Skill: Identify the main idea and details
Writing: Write an essay about a struggle
Life Skill: Read a chart

Before You Read

"The Struggle to Be an All-American Girl" is an essay written by a Chinese American woman. An essay is a nonfiction piece in which an author writes about a subject, usually from a personal point of view. Essays are often fairly short.

The author of this essay, Elizabeth Wong, was the child of an immigrant family. In the essay, she tells how she was torn between her new American life and her family's ties to Chinese ways.

If you have a purpose in mind while you read, you will understand the reading more fully. Before you read the essay, **set a purpose** for your reading. What do you think you will learn? What would you like to know? Write your purpose or purposes on the lines below.

_____

_____

Preview the Reading

Preview "The Struggle to Be an All-American Girl" by looking at the pictures. Then read the first two paragraphs of the essay. Can you tell what it is about?

_____

_____

▶ **Use the Strategy**

On page 128, you set a purpose for your reading. Remember your purpose as you read. Keep in mind what you think you will learn or what you hope to find out.

The Struggle to Be an All-American Girl

Elizabeth Wong

It's still there, the Chinese school on Yale Street where my brother and I used to go. Despite the new coat of paint and the high wire fence, the school I knew 10 years ago remains remarkably, stoically[1] the same.

Every day at 5 P.M., instead of playing with our fourth- and fifth-grade friends or sneaking out to the empty lot to hunt ghosts and animal bones, my brother and I had to go to Chinese school. No amount of kicking, screaming, or pleading could dissuade my mother. She was solidly determined to have us learn the language of our heritage.[2]

Forcibly, she walked us the seven long, hilly blocks from our home to school, setting our defiant tearful faces before the stern principal. My only memory of him is that he swayed on his heels like a palm tree, and he always clasped his impatient twitching hands behind his back. I saw him as a repressed crazy child killer. I knew that if we ever saw his hands we'd be in big trouble.

We all sat in little chairs in an empty auditorium. The room smelled like Chinese medicine, an imported faraway mustiness. Like ancient mothballs or dirty closets. I hated that smell. I favored crisp new scents. Like the soft French perfume that my American teacher wore in public school.

---

1. **stoically:** not affected by outside forces.
2. **heritage:** traditions and culture passed down by earlier generations.

There was a stage far to the right, flanked by an American flag and the flag of the Nationalist Republic of China, which was also red, white, and blue but not as pretty.

Although the emphasis at the school was mainly language—speaking, reading, writing—the lessons always began with an exercise in politeness. With the entrance of the teacher, the best student would tap a bell. Everyone would get up, kowtow,[3] and chant, "Sing san ho," the phonetic[4] for "How are you, teacher?"

Being 10 years old, I had better things to learn than ideographs[5] copied carefully in lines that ran from right to left from the tip of a *moc but,* a real ink pen that had to be held in an awkward way if blotches were to be avoided. After all, I could do the multiplication tables, name the satellites of Mars, and write reports on *Little Women* and *Black Beauty.* Nancy Drew, my favorite book heroine, never spoke Chinese.

Have you learned what you wanted to know? What else would you like to learn about Elizabeth Wong's childhood?

◀ Check-in

The language was a source of embarrassment. More times than not, I had tried to detach myself from the nagging, loud voice that followed me wherever I wandered in the nearby American supermarket outside Chinatown. The voice belonged to my grandmother. She was a fragile woman in her seventies who could outshout the best of the street vendors. Her humor was raunchy, her Chinese rhythmless, patternless. It was quick, it was loud, it was unbeautiful. It was not like the quiet, lilting romance of French or the gentle refinement of the American South. Chinese sounded common. Public.

In Chinatown, the comings and goings of hundreds of Chinese on their daily tasks sounded frenzied. I did not want to be thought of as mad, as talking gibberish. When I spoke English, people nodded at me, smiled sweetly, and said encouraging words. Even

---

3. kowtow: show respect by bowing deeply.
4. phonetic: English spelling of Chinese words based on speech sounds.
5. ideographs: picture-like symbols used in Chinese writing.

the people in my culture would cluck and say that I'd do well in life. "My, doesn't she move her lips fast," they would say, meaning that I'd be able to keep up with the world outside Chinatown.

My brother was even more fanatical than I about speaking English. He was especially hard on my mother. He criticized her, often cruelly, for her pidgin speech—bits of Chinese scattered like chop suey in her conversation. "It's not 'What it is,' Mom," he'd say in exasperation. "It's 'What *is* it, what *is* it, what *is* it!'" Sometimes Mom might leave out an occasional "the" or "a," or perhaps a verb of being. He would stop her in midsentence: "Say it again, Mom. Say it right." When he tripped over his own tongue, he'd blame it on her: "See, Mom, it's all your fault. You set a bad example."

What angered my mother most was when my brother cornered her on her consonants, especially "r." My father had played a cruel joke on Mom. He had assigned her an American name that her tongue wouldn't allow her to say. No matter how hard she tried, "Ruth" always ended up "Luth" or "Roof."

After two years of writing with a *moc but* and reciting words with multiples of meanings, I finally was granted a cultural divorce. I was permitted to stop Chinese school.

I thought of myself as multicultural. I preferred tacos to egg rolls; I enjoyed Cinco de Mayo[6] more than Chinese New Year.

At last, I was one of you; I wasn't one of them.

Sadly, I still am.

---

6. **Cinco de Mayo:** the fifth of May, a Mexican holiday.

 Final Check-in
Did you accomplish your purpose for reading? What else did you learn about growing up as a Chinese American?

Where Immigrants Come From

Where do U.S. immigrants come from? They come from all over the world. But since 1971, a great many people have come from the four countries in the chart below. Notice that the numbers in the first two columns are for decades (10 years). The numbers in the last three columns are for single years.

U.S. Immigrants: Selected Countries Since 1971					
Country of Birth	1971-80	1981-90	1991	1992	1993
China and Taiwan	203,000	389,000	46,000	55,000	80,000
Mexico	637,000	1,653,000	946,000	214,000	127,000
Philippines	360,000	495,000	64,000	61,000	64,000
Vietnam	180,000	401,000	55,000	78,000	60,000

Source: Statistical Abstract of the United States 1994 and 1995

Notice that more immigrants came from Mexico than from any other country. Why do you think this is so? Why do you think so many immigrants from Vietnam came to the U.S. in the early 1990s?

After You Read

A. Comprehension Check

1. The author and her brother hated
   (1) going to Chinese school
   (2) their mother
   (3) Chinese food
   (4) living in Chinatown

2. What did their mother want them to do?
   (1) get more exercise
   (2) teach the Chinese language
   (3) learn the Chinese language
   (4) be punished by the principal

3. What embarrassed Elizabeth Wong?
   (1) Chinese clothes
   (2) the Chinese language
   (3) the family's poverty
   (4) her failure to learn Chinese

4. At the end of the story, what do you think Wong meant when she wrote, "Sadly, I still am"?
   (1) She's sorry that she is not more a part of the Chinese culture.
   (2) She's sad that she is Chinese.
   (3) She wishes she were an American.
   (4) She doesn't want to go to Chinese school.

B. Revisit the Reading Strategy
Think about the purpose or purposes you set before you began reading the essay. Then answer the questions below.

Yes	No	Partly	
_____	_____	_____	I learned what I wanted to know.
_____	_____	_____	I learned other things I didn't expect to learn.

Two facts or ideas I learned: _____

_____

C. Think Beyond the Reading
Think about these questions and discuss them with a partner. Answer the questions in writing if you wish.

- Should newcomers try to hold onto their culture? Why or why not?
- Why do children often learn new ways more easily than their parents? Should they teach their parents? Why or why not?

Think About It: Identify the Main Idea and Details

As you learned in Lesson 1, identifying the main idea and supporting details can help you understand what you read. The **main idea** is what a reading passage is generally about. The **details** provide specific facts, examples, or reasons that support or explain the main idea.

A. Look at Identifying the Main Idea and Details

In paragraphs, a writer often states the main idea in a topic sentence. The topic sentence is often the first or second sentence. The rest of the paragraph includes details that support or give more information about the main idea. In the paragraph below, the topic sentence is underlined. The rest of the paragraph contains details that support it.

> ▶ <u>My brother was even more fanatical than I about speaking English.</u> He was especially hard on my mother. He criticized her, often cruelly, for her pidgin speech—bits of Chinese scattered like chop suey in her conversation. "It's not 'What it is,' Mom," he'd say in exasperation. "It's 'What *is* it, what *is* it, what *is* it!'"

Sometimes the main idea is not stated directly in a sentence. Then you must infer the main idea. Look at the details for clues about the main idea. Ask yourself, "What is this paragraph or passage all about?" Decide what the main idea is and state it in your own words.

In the paragraph below, the main idea is not stated in a sentence. Decide what the paragraph is about. State the main idea in your own words.

> ▶ Every day at 5 P.M., instead of playing with our fourth- and fifth-grade friends or sneaking out to the empty lot . . . my brother and I had to go to Chinese school. No amount of kicking, screaming, or pleading could dissuade my mother. She was solidly determined to have us learn the language of our heritage.

The paragraph is about the author and her brother having to go to Chinese school. Here is one way to state the main idea: "The children's mother made them go to Chinese school, but they didn't like it." The details tell when they went, how they acted, and why their mother made them go.

B. Practice Read each paragraph and answer the questions.

1. ▶ The language was a source of embarrassment. More times than not, I had tried to detach myself from the nagging, loud voice that followed me wherever I wandered in the nearby American supermarket outside Chinatown. The voice belonged to my grandmother. . . . Her humor was raunchy, her Chinese rhythmless, patternless. It was quick, it was loud, it was unbeautiful. It was not like the quiet, lilting romance of French or the gentle refinement of the American South.

   a. Underline the topic sentence.
   b. Are the details facts, examples, or reasons?

   _____

2. ▶ In Chinatown, the comings and goings of hundreds of Chinese on their daily tasks sounded frenzied. I did not want to be thought of as mad, as talking gibberish. When I spoke English, people nodded at me, smiled sweetly, and said encouraging words. Even the people in my culture would cluck and say that I'd do well in life. "My, doesn't she move her lips fast," they would say, meaning that I'd be able to keep up with the world outside Chinatown.

   What is the main idea of this paragraph?

   _____

3. What is the main idea of Elizabeth Wong's essay?

   _____

    Talk About It
   With a partner, take turns summarizing the essay. Plan your summary by noting important points in the essay:
   • the main idea of the essay
   • the most important details

   Tell your summary to your partner. Have your partner evaluate it by telling you how well you explained the main idea and important details of the essay. Then reverse roles.

Write About It: Write an Essay About a Struggle

In this lesson, you read about a struggle between a mother and daughter over the difference between their old and new cultures. In this activity, you will write about one of your own struggles.

A. Prewriting

1. First, choose a topic. Think of someone you struggled with and what the struggle was about. Here are some ideas:

   • I struggled with my parents about staying in school.

   • I struggled with my children about obeying my rules.

   • I struggled with my spouse about spending too much money.

   Write your topic sentence on separate paper.

2. Next, organize your thoughts. On the left side of the page, list the arguments on your side of the struggle. On the right side, list the arguments on other side. Look at the example below.

My Struggle

Topic: I struggled with my parents about staying in school.

My Side	**My Parents' Side**
• I wanted to get a full-time job.	• They said I would earn more with a high school diploma.
• I thought school subjects weren't important.	• They said a diploma opens doors later.
• I was bored with school.	

B. Writing Write a short essay about your struggle using the ideas you listed.

1. In the first paragraph, write an opening sentence that states the topic of your struggle. Then add details to explain the struggle.

2. In the second paragraph, explain your side of the argument.

3. Write another paragraph explaining the opposing point of view.

4. Write a concluding paragraph that explains the outcome of the struggle.

▶ **Save your draft.** At the end of this unit, you will choose one of your drafts to work with further.

Life Skill: A Closer Look at Reading a Chart

Charts organize information so readers can locate facts quickly. To read a chart, first read the title and the headings of the columns and rows. Columns are read from top to bottom. Rows are read from left to right.

Read the title of the chart below. It tells you that the chart gives information about the continents immigrants to the U.S. come from. The first column lists continents. The other columns give numbers of immigrants for different time periods. Read across a row to find the number of immigrants from a given continent in each period. Read down a column to find the number of immigrants from each continent during a given period.

To locate information on a chart, read across a row and down a column. Read the information at the point where the selected row and column meet. As an example, find how many people immigrated to the U.S. from Asia between 1951 and 1960. Find "Asia" in the first column. Then follow that row across to the column for the years 1951–60 and read the number.

Immigration to U.S. by Continent of Origin				
Continents	1951-60	1961-70	1971-80	1981-90
Asia	153,249	427,642	1,588,178	2,066,455
Africa	14,092	28,954	80,779	192,212
Europe	1,325,727	1,123,492	800,368	705,630
North and South America	996,944	1,716,374	1,982,735	3,580,928

Source: Information Please Almanac, Atlas & Yearbook 1993

You can see that 153,249 people from Asia immigrated in the 1950s.

Practice Answer the questions below.

1. How many people immigrated to the U.S. from Asia in the 1980s? _____

2. How many came from Europe in the 1950s? in the 1980s? _____

3. Which continents show an increase in the number of people moving to

   the U.S.? _____

4. Which continent shows a decrease in immigration to the U.S.? _____

►Writing Skills Mini-Lesson: Combining Ideas

Combining related ideas helps to make your writing smoother and easier to understand. There are several ways to combine ideas.

1. A **simple sentence** contains one complete thought. But a simple sentence can combine related ideas in the form of a **compound subject,** a **compound verb,** or both.

   Simple sentences: Ali is married. Helen is married to Ali.
   Compound subject: **Ali and Helen** are married to each other.

   Simple sentences: They live in the U.S. They work in the U.S.
   Compound verb: They <u>live and work</u> in the U.S.

   Compound subject and verb: **Ali and Helen** <u>live and work</u> in the U.S.

2. A **compound sentence** is made up of two simple sentences. The two sentences are joined by a **comma** plus a **connecting word** such as *and, but, or, yet,* or *so.*

   Simple sentences: Ali speaks Arabic. Helen speaks Greek.
   Compound sentence: Ali speaks Arabic, **and** Helen speaks Greek.

   Simple sentences: Ali doesn't speak Greek. He understands a few words.
   Compound sentence: Ali doesn't speak Greek, **but** he understands a few words.

   Simple sentences: Ali and Helen both speak English. They understand each other.
   Compound sentence: Ali and Helen both speak English, **so** they understand each other.

Practice On separate paper, write one sentence that combines the ideas in each pair of sentences.

1. Ali is originally from Egypt. Helen is from Greece.
2. They were studying in the same community college.
   They were working there, too.
3. Ali worked in the college library. Helen worked in the admissions office.
4. Then Ali and Helen met. They started to eat lunch together often.
5. Ali and Helen fell in love. They got married three years ago.
6. Ali and Helen come from different cultures. They are very close.

Reading Review

Who Are the Immigrants?

We see their faces on the news and in our neighborhoods. They may speak foreign languages. We may not know them very well. We know they often are working hard to make a living and to learn English. Many find their new homeland strange, and even frightening. We know this much, but we can't say much more about them as a group. For the truth is that they are very different from each other. They belong under that umbrella we label *immigrants*. But they are not one group.

National groups differ from each other in language and religious beliefs, in clothing styles, and in tastes in food and music. Their backgrounds are different, too. They came to this country for different reasons. Some came looking for a better chance in life. They brought with them money and personal belongings to start their new lives. But others were forced to leave their homes because of violence and war. Those immigrants, called refugees, left their countries in fear for their lives. Many arrived in the United States without families, and with little more than the clothes on their backs.

Perhaps surprising to some people are the differences that exist *within* other nations or cultures. For instance, some Chinese are Buddhist, while others are Catholic. Some immigrants from the same country don't speak the same language. For example, the Philippine Islands are home to more than 70 different languages! Groups from the same country vary in education and background, too. Many of the first refugees from Vietnam came from the cities and were well educated. But other Vietnamese refugees were poor people from the country who couldn't read or write.

So who are the immigrants? There is no simple answer. We can learn about their many cultures. But we must also know them as individuals.

Choose the best answer to questions 1 and 2 below. Then write answers to questions 3 and 4.

1. What is the main idea of the article?
   (1) All people have things in common.
   (2) Immigrants have many differences.
   (3) Immigrants have many problems.
   (4) Americans have a poor attitude toward immigrants.

2. We can infer that refugees
   (1) are the same as other immigrants
   (2) may need many kinds of help
   (3) planned their move carefully
   (4) don't want to be in the U.S.

3. Name one way in which most immigrants are alike. _____

   _____

4. Name two ways in which immigrants may differ from each other. _____

   _____

   _____

Writing Process

In Unit 4, you wrote three first drafts. Choose the piece that you would like to work with further. You will revise, edit, and make a final copy of this draft.

_____ your fable that taught a lesson (page 118)
_____ your diary entry about a big event in your life (page 126)
_____ your essay about a struggle (page 136)

Find the first draft you chose. Then turn to page 160 in this book. Follow steps 3, 4, and 5 in the Writing Process to create a final draft.

As you revise, check your draft for these specific points:
Fable: Did you include the lesson learned from the experience?
Diary entry: Did you include your feelings about the event?
Essay: Have you explained both sides of the struggle and the outcome?

Skills Review

This Skills Review will let you see how well you can use the skills taught in this book. When you have finished Units 1–4, complete this review. Then share your work with your instructor.

Reading Skills Review

Read each passage and answer the questions that follow.

Beating Budget-Phobia

Jane Bryant Quinn

I learned what a budget could do when I was 25, divorced and supporting a child on insufficient income. I knew I was in trouble when I started shoving unopened bills into a drawer because I couldn't pay them. A budget pulled me out. I discovered that even on my mini-income, I was letting money leak through my fingers.

Budgets do more than drag spending into line with income, however. They're a powerful tool for getting what you want in the future. Since the word *budget* smells of shortages and self-denial, I prefer *spending plan,* which puts you in active control. The only way to get more money for what you want is to spend less on something else. If a budget won't work, try this five-step plan:

List your priorities. What do you need most from your income—a down payment? A rainy-day fund? Debt repayment? Retirement security? More education? Be specific and set a deadline for reaching each goal. For example, you might decide to retire your MasterCard bill in six months, at the rate of $300 a month. When you get paid, that $300 gets spent first. Start with a small goal, then reach for larger ones.

Find out where you stand. Study your check registers, bills and credit-card statements to learn exactly where your money goes. Make a list of expenses on the left side of a page: mortgage, telephone, electricity, auto loan, clothes and so on. Note the amount you spend in each category to the nearest dollar. Then keep track of what you buy for cash for a few weeks and add those to your list: magazines, bus fare, gasoline, movies, hairdresser. Some things may seem too trivial to bother with. But if you can save $5 a day for a year, you'll have $1,825 that could fund an Individual Retirement Account.

Compare your total monthly spending with your disposable income after tax. Never mind if you're in the red; that's the problem you mean to fix.

Decide how you want to spend your money. In a second column, next to your actual expenses, rearrange your spending so it matches your income and provides money for your top-priority goal. It's often better to cut a little from every flexible category rather than to slash just one or two. Reconsider all spending.

Even good plans are not carved in stone. Do you really need a car phone—or even call waiting? Should you switch to low-cost term life insurance?

Try to follow your new spending plan. Keep track of how you do. You won't be completely successful; no one is at first. Make changes as you go along until you have a plan that works. Unexpected expenses arise all the time. That's where your budget becomes a money-management tool. If you have to fix the car this month—and your rainy-day fund won't cover it— your budget will show what other spending can be delayed so the car can be paid for.

Choose the best answer to each question.

1. What is the main idea of this article?
   (1) Find ways to save on household bills.
   (2) A spending plan can put you in control of your spending.
   (3) You need to identify your spending priorities.
   (4) Find ways to earn more money.

2. Most of the details in this article explain
   (1) the author's life and problems
   (2) how to pay off credit card bills
   (3) the importance of goal setting
   (4) how to create a spending plan

3. Electricity would belong in which budget category?

  (1) auto expenses
  (2) household expenses
  (3) holiday gifts
  (4) cash and extras

4. Which of the following is a fact?

  (1) The word *budget* smells of shortages and self-denial.
  (2) Some things may seem too trivial to bother with.
  (3) If you can save $5 a day for a year, you'll have $1,825.
  (4) You won't be completely successful at first.

5. To solve her money problems, the author

  (1) stopped spending so much
  (2) got a better job
  (3) borrowed money
  (4) stopped paying her bills

6. In the five-step plan, before you figure out where your money goes, you should

  (1) try to follow your spending plan
  (2) rearrange your spending
  (3) compare spending with income
  (4) list your priorities and goals

The Work of Many Cultures

The United States has been called a melting pot of different peoples. There are those who believe this diversity is not good for the country. But in fact, the U.S. was built by workers from many cultures. Our way of life is based on the mixing of ethnic and racial groups. Here are just a few examples:

- The 1800s were a time of canal and railroad building. In the eastern half of the U.S., most of this work was done by Irish immigrants.
- Who built the first railroad across the western United States? Nine out of ten of the workers were Chinese.
- About one-third of the cowboys in the cattle crews out west were African Americans and Mexicans.
- In the 1870s, Russian immigrants brought with them a type of winter wheat that boosted wheat production.
- Many Jewish people worked in the garment factories of New York City. By 1900, they were making half of the nation's clothes. Italian women joined them later.

Today, the story is much the same. People from Europe, Asia, Africa, and South America continue to make their homes here. They bring with them a willingness to work and rich cultural backgrounds. All play a part in making our country what it is.

Choose the best answer to each question.

7. Which of the following is an opinion?
   (1) Diversity is not good for our country.
   (2) Many Jewish people worked in garment factories.
   (3) Irish workers helped build the canals.
   (4) Many railroad workers were Chinese.

8. In this article, you can infer that without its racial and ethnic groups
   (1) our country would not exist
   (2) our country would not have railroads
   (3) our country would not be as rich
   (4) our country would not have workers

Women at Work

Women have always worked. They have been partners in running the family farm or business. They have cooked, cleaned, and cared for their families. These days many women also work outside the home. By 1990, more than half of all women were working or looking for jobs. And 79 percent of women with children under age 3 had jobs.

What work do women do? Some are lawyers, engineers, and police officers. Many work in service areas. They are bank tellers, hairdressers, and nurses. Service jobs like these are often seen as "women's work." A growing number of women are business owners. In 1987, outside of farming, nearly one-third of all one-owner businesses were owned by women. On top of it all, most women still do most of the household chores and have responsibility for child care.

The following circle graph shows the different types of businesses owned by women. Each section shows the percent of women business owners who own that type of business. For example, 24 percent of all female business owners have wholesale or retail trade businesses.

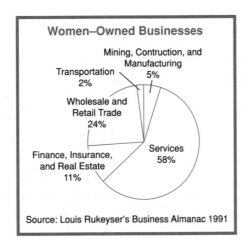

Women–Owned Businesses

Mining, Contruction, and Manufacturing 5%

Transportation 2%

Wholesale and Retail Trade 24%

Finance, Insurance, and Real Estate 11%

Services 58%

Source: Louis Rukeyser's Business Almanac 1991

Choose the best answer to each question.

9. According to the graph, more women own businesses in the area of
   (1) services than all others combined
   (2) transportation than trade
   (3) mining, construction, and manufacturing than trade
   (4) transportation than finance, insurance, and real estate

10. From the article, you can infer that women
    (1) stay home more now
    (2) no longer care for their families
    (3) are doing more work now than ever before
    (4) own fewer businesses than in the past

Writing Skills Review

On separate paper, copy the paragraph, correcting errors in capitalization, punctuation, and subject-verb agreement.

We all have habits we want to break, but habits are not always bad. What if we all got in the habit of helping? Even small good deeds makes a difference. What can you do. You can read a story to a child or you can help your husband or wife with a chore. Don't wait for valentine's day to say, "i love you." You might give someone a hug or you could offer a word of praise. You can take time to listen. Both adults and children needs a friendly ear. Your time and attention is sometimes the best gifts you can give. You should practice smiling, too. People will smile back.

Write About It

On separate paper, write about the topic below. Use the Revising Checklist below to check your draft. Follow the first four steps of the Writing Process (page 160) to write, revise, and edit your draft. Then write a final draft and share it with your instructor.

Topic: Write two paragraphs about your favorite job. In the first paragraph, describe the job and tell why it's your favorite job. In the second paragraph, describe the skills needed to do the job well.

Revising Checklist

Revise your draft. Check that your draft

_____ has one main idea in each paragraph

_____ includes details that describe your favorite job

_____ includes details that describe the skills needed to do the job well

_____ includes details that explain why each skill is important

Skills Review Answers

Reading Skills

1. (2)	**6.** (4)
2. (4)	**7.** (1)
3. (2)	**8.** (3)
4. (3)	**9.** (1)
5. (1)	**10.** (3)

Writing Skills

There is more than one way to correct some of the errors. Here is one way.

We all have habits we want to break, but habits are not always bad. What if we all got in the habit of helping? Even small good deeds make a difference. What can you do? You can read a story to a child, or you can help your husband or wife with a chore. Don't wait for Valentine's Day to say, "I love you." You might give someone a hug, or you could offer a word of praise. You can take time to listen. Both adults and children need a friendly ear. Your time and attention are sometimes the best gifts you can give. You should practice smiling, too. People will smile back.

Write About It

When you feel confident about your final draft, share it with your instructor.

Evaluation Chart

Check your Skills Review answers. On the chart below, circle the number of any answer you missed. You may need to review the lesson(s) indicated next to that question number.

Question	Skill	Lessons
1	identify main idea and details	1, 12
2	identify main idea and details	1, 12
3	categorize information	2, 8
4	identify facts and opinions	6, 9
5	recognize problems and solutions	3
6	follow steps in a process	5
7	identify facts and opinions	6, 9
8	make inferences	4, 11
9	compare and contrast	10
10	make inferences	4, 11

▶ **Go on to page 148** to complete Student Self-Assessment #2.

Student Self-Assessment #2

After you finish the Skills Preview, do this self-assessment.
Share your responses with your instructor.

Reading	Good at this	Need help	Don't know how to do this
I can read and understand			
1. stories, poems, biographies, fables, and essays			
2. articles in magazines, newspapers, and books			
3. forms, applications, checks, and bank statements			
4. charts and graphs; signs and symbols			
5. diagrams and maps			
6. memos, letters, and diary entries			
7. brochures and announcements			
When I read, I can			
1. figure out new words by using context clues			
2. use what I already know to help me understand			
3. set a purpose for reading			
4. skim to get a general idea of the reading material			
5. identify main ideas and details, problems and solutions			
6. categorize information			
7. make inferences			
8. follow steps in a process			
9. recognize facts and opinions			
10. summarize what I've read			
11. try to predict what is coming next			
12. compare and contrast information			

Writing	Good at this	Need help	Don't know how to do this
I can fill out or write			
1. an action plan and instructions			
2. forms and applications; memos and letters			
3. paragraphs with a topic sentence and supporting details			
4. short articles, personal accounts, and diary entries			
5. an autobiography; fables; essays			
When I write, I can			
1. think of good ideas and organize them			
2. use facts, examples, or reasons to support my main ideas			
3. express myself clearly so others understand			
4. revise my writing to improve it			
5. edit my writing to correct spelling, capitalization, punctuation, and usage errors			
6. make subjects and verbs agree			
7. combine related ideas			

Answer Key

When sample answers are given, your answers may use different wording, but they should be similar to the sample answers.

Unit 1 Money Matters

▼ Lesson 1

After You Read (p. 19)
A. 1. (4)
   2. (2)
   3. (3)
   4. (1)
   5. (3)

Think About It: Identify the Main Idea and Details (p. 20)
B. Practice
1. Main idea sentence to be underlined:
   Some bills can be eliminated altogether.
Sample answer:
You can get rid of some bills altogether.
2. Main idea sentence to be underlined:
   Sadly, the pleasure that comes from extravagances often disappears long before the bills do.
Sample answer:
The fun of buying expensive things is over long before you stop paying for them.
3. Main idea sentence to be underlined:
   The costliest money trap is the credit-card bill that's never paid off.
   Any one of the following details is correct:
   Minimum payments are as low as 2 percent of the total bill.
   It can take more than 11 years to pay off a $2,000 bill.
   Many people pay only the minimum each month.
   Some people have 10 or 12 different credit card accounts.

Life Skill: A Closer Look at Reading a Circle Graph (p. 23)
Practice
1. 16%

2. 10%
3. 58%

▼ Lesson 2

After You Read (p. 27)
A. 1. Personal Checking, EARN
   2. $ 3.00
   3. $750.00
   4. 2%
   5. the Deposit Account Regulations
   6. their Social Security numbers
B. 1. automated teller machine
   2. Answers will vary.

Think About It: Understand Categories (p. 28)
Practice
1. *Benefits* category *or* the middle column
2. *Plan* category *or* the first column
3. *Fees* category *or* the third column
4. Housing
5. Personal Taxes

Life Skill: Read a Bank Statement (p. 31)
Practice
1. $50.00
2. $1,135.60
3. Carol Ramirez made a deposit of $327.12.
4. $1,748.56

▼ Lesson 3

After You Read (p. 37)
A. 1. (1)
   2. (3)
   3. (4)
   4. (2)

Think About It: Recognize Problems and Solutions (p. 38)
B. Practice
1. . . . the Leets had seen that billions of dollars pouring into Third World welfare programs were not reaching those who needed help.
Sample answers:
2. Give a little money to start small businesses and let people help themselves.
3. a. Pilar Moya thought she couldn't start a business.
3. b. Pilar Moya joined with others to start a bakery.

Life Skill: Understand a Budget (p. 41)
Practice
1. $265
2. $240
3. yes
4. $1,500
5. yes
6. housing and insurance
7. They are set amounts.
8. Spending in those areas varies.

▼ Writing Skills Mini-Lesson: Capitalization Rules (p. 42)
Practice
When I shop, I always compare prices. For example, I usually use Tide for my wash, but last Monday I got Ivory since it was on sale. I also compare prices for services. When I moved to Chicago last April, my friend Jamal told me about two good doctors. I chose Dr. Angela Carter at Grant Hospital because she charges less than the other doctor.

▼ Unit 1 Review (p. 43)
Reading Review
1. (2)
2. (1)
3. (2)
4. (3)

Unit 2 On the Job

▼ Lesson 4
After You Read (p. 49)
A. 1. He is a cabdriver.
2. Choose any two answers: carry her bags, open her door, set her bags inside, turn on the lamp, untie her coat
3. 5 times
Sample answers:
4. Myrtle raises three children.
5. She puts the newspapers in plastic bags so they don't get wet.

Think About It: Make Inferences (p. 50)
B. Practice
Sample answers:
1. a. She probably lives alone.
   b. There were probably quite a few steps to climb.
   c. She is lonely and wants attention. She is frail and cannot do some things for herself.
2. a. It is a time to plan her day. It's good exercise. She needs a break from her children.
   b. He was impressed that she came rain or shine and took pride in her work.

Life Skill: Read Workplace Signs and Symbols (p. 54)
Practice
Sample answers:
1. You could come into contact with dangerous chemicals or other substances.
2. Only certain people have the right to come in here.
3. Be careful in front of this door because the door or a person might bump into you.
4. Be careful because there are electrical power lines in this area.
5. To avoid hurting yourself, use your legs, not your back, to lift.
6. Wear a hard hat to protect your head in this area.
7. Be careful because this liquid can catch fire.
8. Walk carefully.
9. This floor becomes slippery when it is wet.
10. You must show a permit or a badge to come in here.
11. You must wear safety glasses here to protect your eyes.
12. Smoking is not allowed here.
13. People in wheelchairs can get around here.

▼ Lesson 5

After You Read (p. 59)
A. 1. (2)
2. (4)
3. (3)
4. (4)

Think About It: Follow Steps in a Process (p. 60)
B. Practice
1. Remove the stem assembly.
2. Put back the stem assembly.
3. faucet handle, decorative cover
4. 2, 1, 3
5. 2. Replace the packing nut by turning it clockwise with a wrench.
   3. Replace the decorative cover, if any.
   4. Replace the faucet handle, if it was removed to uncover the packing nut.

Life Skill: Read a Diagram (p. 63)
Practice
1. B
2. 2
Sample answers:
3. It shows how to attach the connectors, part D.
4. The bolts attach part D to the legs and top support and also to the legs and base support. *or* The bolts attach part D to parts A and C and parts B and C.
5. The screws attach the glass supports to the legs and the top. *or* The screws attach the glass supports to parts A and C.
6. They are shaped the same. *or*
   They are both supports. *or*
   They both attach to the legs and connectors.

▼ Lesson 6

After You Read (p. 68)
A. Sample answers:
1. oil spills on the floor and in the storage area
2. They think it will help employees to work smarter.
   They think it will help solve safety problems.
   They want employees to learn new skills.
3. to encourage more people to sign up for the course

4. Employees found solutions to the safety problem.
5. Answers will vary.
B. Other: meeting time, who should attend the meeting.

Think About It: Identify Facts and Opinions (p. 69)
B. Practice

1. O	6. O
2. F	7. F
3. F	8. O
4. O	9. F
5. F	10. O

Life Skill: Read a Time Sheet and an Invoice (p. 72)
A. Practice
1. payroll personnel in the office
2. 8 hours and 9 minutes *or* 8.25 hours
3. 1 hour
4. P. Morissard

B. Practice
5. $115.49
6. charged on VISA
7. 8504
8. 6–10
9. $15.95
10. $31.90

▼ Writing Skills Mini-Lesson: Making Subjects and Verbs Agree (p. 74)
Practice
Sample answers:
1. Carpenters build cabinets and furniture.
2. A photographer takes pictures.
3. A driving instructor teaches people how to drive.
4. Pilots fly planes.
5. Firefighters put out fires.
6. I am a student.

▼ Unit 2 Review (p. 75)
Reading Review
1. (1)
2. (2)
3. (4)
4. (1)

Unit 3 Making a Difference

▼ Lesson 7

After You Read (p. 83)

A. Sample answers:
1. She was a woman.
   She was black.
   She was very small.
   Her family was poor.
2. He took her to political meetings with him. *or*
   He encouraged her to ask questions and learn. *or*
   He had the children read and discuss the newspaper every day.
3. the U.S. House of Representatives *or* the U.S. Congress
4. women and minorities

Think About It: Summarize Information (p. 84)

B. Practice
1. Sample answers:
   -1942 went to Brooklyn College
   -joined the debate club in college and gave speeches
   -taught nursery school
   -got a master's degree in early childhood education from Columbia University
   -married Conrad Chisholm
   -joined a Democratic club
   -formed another club with other minority members and helped an African American candidate win an election
2. Sample answers:
   -1964 was elected to the New York state assembly
   -was discriminated against because she was a woman
   -1968 won election to the U.S. Congress and became first black woman member of Congress
   -elected to Congress seven times
   -1972 ran for president of the U.S.
   -opened the way for women and minorities

3. Sample Summary:
   In 1942, Shirley entered Brooklyn College. There she joined the debate club and became an experienced speaker. After college she taught nursery school and earned a master's degree from Columbia University. She married Conrad Chisholm and became active in politics. She joined a Democratic club but wasn't allowed to make decisions. She formed another club with other minority members and helped an African American candidate win an election.
   In 1964, Shirley Chisholm ran for the New York state assembly and won by a landslide. She said that she met with more discrimination because she was a woman than because she was African American. In 1968, she was elected to the U.S. Congress, becoming the first black woman member of Congress. In 1972 she ran for president. She was not nominated, but her career opened the way for other women and minorities.

Life Skill: Read a Brochure (p. 87)

Practice
Sample answers:
1. Parents should be nonviolent so their children will learn nonviolent behavior.
2. What: parenting classes
   When: first and third Tuesday of each month, 7:00–8:00 P.M.
   Where: St. Joseph Hospital, Room 202
3. Call 555-3482
4. Sample answer:
   so the organizers will know how many people to expect

▼ Lesson 8

After You Read (p. 91)

A. 1. (3)
   2. (1)
   3. (4)
   4. (1)
   5. birthdate, birthplace, home address, sex

Think About It: Categorize Information (p. 92)
Practice
1. Sworn Statement and Signature
2. Residence Information
3. Eligibility: Right to Vote

Life Skill: Read Community Announcements (p. 95)
Practice
Sample answers:
1. What: A Business Meeting of the Hillsboro City School Board
   When: September 21 at 7:30 P.M.
   Where: Ford Middle School
2. Changes related to the Code of Conduct; a new representative to the Parent Advisory Council
3. Watch it on television September 22 at 7 P.M. on Channel 2

▼ **Lesson 9**

After You Read (p. 100)
A. 1. (2)
   2. (1)
   3. (4)
   4. (3)

Think About It: Identify Facts and Opinions (p. 101)
B. **Practice**
1. O   6. F
2. F   7. O
3. F   8. O
4. O   9. O
5. O   10. F

Life Skill: A Closer Look at a Bar Graph (p. 104)
A. **Practice**
1. religious organizations
2. 15 percent
B. **Practice**
3. 225
4. about 200

Sample answers:
5. Students in both grades who read for fun scored higher on the test.
6. Children who read for fun are better readers than those who don't. *or*
   Good readers read for fun more often than other readers.

▼ **Writing Skills Mini-Lesson: More on Making Subjects and Verbs Agree (p. 106)**
Practice
1. My wife and I are the parents of twin daughters.
2. Our daughters and their best friend go to Ray School.
3. Selena and Cristina are in the second grade.
4. The association of parents and teachers is active at Ray.
5. The teachers at Ray School work well with the parents.
6. Every parent of young children needs to join the PTA.

▼ **Unit 3 Review (p. 107)**
Reading Review
1. (1)
2. 3 a.
   1 b.
   4 c.
   2 d.
3. a. O   d. F
   b. O   e. F
   c. O   f. O

Unit 4 Many Cultures

▼ **Lesson 10**

After You Read (p. 115)
A. 1. (2)
   2. (4)
   3. (2)
   4. (1)

Think About It: Compare and Contrast (p. 116)
B. Practice
Sample answers:
1. Each has a similar moral: Pride comes before a fall. *or*
   In each, a land animal is dissatisfied with his life and wants to be high like an eagle.
2. Different: The pigeon-hawk chats with his friends and flies around, but the hare takes a nap.
   Similar: Both the hare and the pigeon-hawk think they will easily win.
3. Both are about a race between animals. *or*
   In both, the faster animal loses and the slower animal wins. *or*
   Both have a similar lesson: Slow and steady wins the race. *or*
   In both, the faster animal is overconfident.
4. Similar: Both have a tortoise and a bird as characters.
   Different: The tortoise loses in one and wins in the other.
5. They believe in similar morals. *or*
   They observe similar traits in human nature. *or*
   They use tales to teach lessons.

Life Skill: Read a Map (p. 119)
Practice
1. North America, South America, Europe, Africa, Asia, Antarctica, Australia (in any order)
2. Europe
3. the Arctic Ocean
4. the Atlantic Ocean
5. Europe
6. Australia

▼ Lesson 11

After You Read (p. 123)
A. 1. any two of the following: Rose; store windows where dolls move; Rockefeller Center; a big green tree; an orchestra of 500 people
   2. the New Year

3. any three of the following: family and friends; food; staying up and eating all night long; a big green tree; watching the president on TV; hearing the Soviet hymn; standing to meet the New Year; watching TV all night long; all the songs, the music, the people
Sample answers:
   4. she would know the American songs
   5. The sentiments are the same.

Think About It: Make Inferences (p. 124)
B. Practice
Sample answers:
1. a. She noticed them because she had not seen anything like them before. *or*
      She liked the dolls and wanted to have one.
   b. The dolls might have been puppets. *or*
      They might be figures representing people in Christmas scenes.
2. a Christmas tree
3. She thinks they are similar in important ways. Even if American songs someday take the place of Russian songs, there will always be a celebration with singing and music.

Life Skill: Read a Schedule (p. 127)
Practice
1. Monday through Thursday, 6:30–9:00 P.M., in Room 101B
2. Tuesday and Thursday, 7:00–9:00 P.M.
3. morning: T. Feng
   evening: H. Ruiz
4. Tuesday and Thursday, 7:00–9:00 P.M., in Room 105
5. M. Danner, in Room 201A

▼ Lesson 12

After You Read (p. 133)
A. 1. (1)
   2. (3)
   3. (2)
   4. (1)

Think About It: Identify the Main Idea and Details (p. 134)

B. Practice

1. a. The language was a source of embarrassment.
   b. The details are reasons.

Sample answers:

2. Elizabeth wanted to speak English rather than Chinese.

3. As a child, Elizabeth Wong hated Chinese school and wanted to be more American, but as an adult she is sorry that she is not more Chinese.

Life Skill: A Closer Look at Reading a Chart (p. 137)

Practice

1. 2,066,455
2. in the 1950s: 1,325,727; in the 1980s: 705,630
3. Asia, Africa, and North and South America
4. Europe

▼ **Writing Skills Mini-Lesson: Combining Ideas (p. 138)**

There is more than one correct way to combine these sentences. Sample answers:

1. Ali is originally from Egypt, and Helen is from Greece. *or*
   Ali is originally from Egypt, but Helen is from Greece.

2. They were studying and working in the same community college.

3. Ali worked in the college library, and Helen worked in the admissions office. *or*
   Ali worked in the college library, but Helen worked in the admissions office.

4. Then Ali and Helen met and started to eat lunch together often.

5. Ali and Helen fell in love, and they got married three years ago.

6. Ali and Helen come from different cultures, but they are very close. *or*
   Ali and Helen come from different cultures, yet they are very close.

▼ **Unit 4 Review (p. 139)**

Reading Review

1. (2)
2. (2)

Sample answers:

3. They work hard to learn English and make a living.
   They may find this country strange and frightening.

4. Any two of the following: language; religion; education; clothing; food; music; background and reasons for coming to America.

Writing Skills

This handbook reviews the rules you learned in the Writing Skills Mini-Lessons in this book.

Capitalization Rules

Use a **capital letter** at the beginning of these words:

1. **The first word of a sentence and the word *I*.**

    My husband and **I** want a car. **We** are saving for a new one.

2. **Days of the week, holidays, and months.**

    Tuesday, Saturday, Thanksgiving, the **Fourth** of **July, March, June**

> **Tip** Do not capitalize small words like *the, a, of,* or *and* unless they come at the beginning of a sentence.

3. **Names of places such as cities, states, countries, and continents.**

    Detroit, Michigan, Japan, Europe

4. **Names of organizations, institutions, companies, and brands.**

    American Cancer Society, University of Delaware, Ford Motor Company, Kleenex

5. **People's titles and names.**

    Mr. Martin Pagano, Ms. Carla Raymundo, Mrs. Vista, Ted Beck, Dr. Albert Choi, Professor Sykes, Senator Feinstein

> **Tip** Capitalize people's titles only when they are used with the person's name. Do not capitalize them when they appear alone: I like **Professor Rashid.** She is an excellent **professor.**

Making Subjects and Verbs Agree

Every sentence has a **subject** (who or what the sentence is about) and a **verb** (what the subject does or is). In the present tense, verbs appear in different forms. The form of a verb changes depending on its subject. In other words, a verb must **agree** with its subject.

Follow these rules to make subjects and verbs agree in the present tense:

1. **Add the *s* or *es* ending to the verb when the subject is a *singular noun* or the pronouns *he, she,* or *it*.**
   A **carpenter** builds cabinets. **He** builds cabinets.
   A **pilot** flies planes. **She** flies planes.

2. **Do *not* add an ending to the verb when the subject is a *plural noun* or the pronouns *I, you, we,* or *they*.**
   Carpenters build cabinets. **I** build cabinets. **You** build cabinets.
   They build cabinets. **We** all build cabinets.

3. **The verb *to be* has several forms. See the chart below.**

• I am	• we are
• you are	• you are
• he is, she is, it is	• they are
• the car is, the pilot is	• the cars are, the pilots are

   I am glad you got a new job.
   Are you pleased, too?
   It is a good job.

   We are happy for you.
   You are anxious to start your new job.
   Good **jobs are** hard to find.

More on Making Subjects and Verbs Agree

Verbs must agree with their subjects. Pay particular attention to this rule when you write in the **present tense.** Watch out for these tricky situations.

1. **Compound subjects.** You can join two singular subjects with the word *and* to make a compound subject. A compound subject is plural, so don't add *s* to a present tense verb. For the verb *to be,* use *are.*

   Singular
   Subject   Verb

   Alonso wants to join the Parent Teacher Association.

   Compound
   Subject   Verb

   Alonso and Leticia want to join the PTA.

   Singular
   Subject Verb

   My wife is a member of the PTA.

   Compound
   Subject   Verb

   My wife and I are members of the PTA.

2. **Interrupting words.** Sometimes a group of words comes between the subject and the verb. To choose the correct present tense verb form, look back to the subject and ignore the interrupting words.

   Singular
   Subject   Verb

   The **teacher** of our twin daughters **is** new.

   Plural
   Subject   Verb

   Parents who are active in the school **help** all the children.

   Singular Subject   Verb

   The **Parent Teacher Association** at our school **is** very active.

   Plural
   Subject   Verb

   All the **children** in the school **benefit** from the work of the PTA.

Combining Ideas

Combining related ideas helps to make your writing smoother and easier to understand. There are several ways to combine ideas.

1. A **simple sentence** contains one complete thought. But a simple sentence can combine related ideas in the form of a **compound subject,** a **compound verb,** or both.
   Simple sentences: Ali is married. Helen is married.
   Compound subject: **Ali and Helen** are married.

   Simple sentences: They live in the United States. They work in the United States.
   Compound verb: They **live and work** in the United States.

   Compound subject and verb: **Ali and Helen live and work** in the United States.

2. A **compound sentence** is made up of two simple sentences. The two sentences are joined by a **comma** plus a **connecting word** such as *and, but, or, yet,* or *so.*
   Simple sentences: Ali speaks Arabic. Helen speaks Greek.
   Compound sentence: Ali speaks Arabic, **and** Helen speaks Greek.

   Simple sentences: Ali doesn't speak Greek. He understands a few words.
   Compound sentence: Ali doesn't speak Greek, **but** he understands a few words.

   Simple sentences: Ali and Helen both speak English. They understand each other.
   Compound sentence: Ali and Helen both speak English, **so** they understand each other.

   Simple sentences: Ali and Helen both worked at the community college. They didn't know each other.
   Compound sentence: Ali and Helen both worked at the community college, **yet** they didn't know each other.

   Simple sentences: Helen can speak English. She can speak Greek if you wish.
   Compound sentence: Helen can speak English, **or** she can speak Greek if you wish.

The Writing Process

The Writing Process is a series of stages that can help you create
a good piece of writing. These stages are shown below.

1. Prewrite, or plan your writing.
 A. Think about your topic.
 B. List ideas about your topic.

 C. Organize your ideas.
 • Decide which ideas you will use.
 • Decide how you will order them.

2. Write a first draft.
 A. Use your ideas from stage 1.

 B. Write about your topic.
 • Clearly state your main ideas.
 • Give appropriate facts, examples, or
 reasons to support your main idea.

3. Revise your first draft.
 A. Check that your draft
 _____ includes your important ideas
 _____ develops the topic with
 appropriate facts, examples,
 or reasons
 _____ is clear and easy to understand

 B. Make changes to improve your
 writing.
 • You can add, cross out, or move
 information.
 • You can reword sentences.

4. Edit your work.
 A. Check your draft for errors in
 _____ complete sentences
 _____ correct spelling
 _____ correct punctuation
 _____ correct capitalization
 _____ correct usage

 B. Correct any mistakes you find.
 If you need help, use the Writing Skills
 Handbook on page 156 or ask your
 instructor.

5. Recopy your draft.
 A. Write a final draft. Include all
 of your revising and editing
 changes.
 B. Compare your first and final drafts.
 Note improvements.

 C. Share your final draft with a classmate,
 a friend, or your instructor.